# CRITICAL TOOLS FOR THE STUDY OF THE NEW TESTAMENT

# CRITICAL TOOLS FOR THE STUDY OF THE NEW TESTAMENT

Watson E. Mills

Mellen Biblical Press Series
Volume 47

MELLEN BIBLICAL PRESS
Lewiston/Queenston/Lampeter

Library of Congress Cataloging-in-Publication Data

Mills, Watson E.
    Critical tools for the study of the New Testament / Watson E.
Mills.
        p.    cm. -- (Mellen Biblical Press series ; v. 47)
    Includes and index.
    ISBN 0-7734-2405-9 (hardcover)
    1. Bible. N.T.--Criticism, interpretation, etc.--Bibliography.
I. Title. II. Series.
Z7772.L1M549   1995
[BS2330.2)]
016.225--dc20                                                95-31314
                                                                CIP

This is volume 47 in the continuing series
Mellen Biblical Press Series
Volume 47  ISBN 0-7734-2405-9
MBP Series ISBN 0-7734-2430-X

A CIP catalog record for this book is available from the British Library.

All rights reserved. For information contact

The Edwin Mellen Press                  The Edwin Mellen Press
        Box 450                                    Box 67
Lewiston, New York                       Queenston, Ontario
   USA  14092-0450                         CANADA  L0S 1L0

The Edwin Mellen Press, Ltd.
Lampeter, Dyfed, Wales
UNITED KINGDOM  SA48 7DY

Printed in the United States of America

# Dedication

*to Irene H. Palmer*

*friend, co-worker, counselor, confidant,*
*advisor, listener, defender, and loyal supporter*

# Table of Contents

Preface . . . . . . . . . . . . . . . . . . . . . . . . . . . . . . . . . . . . . . . . . . . . ix

Chapter 1  Abbreviations . . . . . . . . . . . . . . . . . . . . . . . . . . . . . . . 1

Chapter 2  Bibliographies . . . . . . . . . . . . . . . . . . . . . . . . . . . . . . 15

Chapter 3  Periodicals . . . . . . . . . . . . . . . . . . . . . . . . . . . . . . . . 33

Chapter 4  Indexing and Abstracting . . . . . . . . . . . . . . . . . . . . . 39

Chapter 5  Book Reviews . . . . . . . . . . . . . . . . . . . . . . . . . . . . . . 45

Chapter 6  Dissertations and Theses . . . . . . . . . . . . . . . . . . . . . 49

Chapter 7  Dictionaries . . . . . . . . . . . . . . . . . . . . . . . . . . . . . . . 53

Chapter 8  Commentaries . . . . . . . . . . . . . . . . . . . . . . . . . . . . . . 61

Chapter 9  Archaeology and Geography . . . . . . . . . . . . . . . . . . . 79

Chapter 10  Texts of the New Testament . . . . . . . . . . . . . . . . . . . 83

Chapter 11  Grammars . . . . . . . . . . . . . . . . . . . . . . . . . . . . . . . . 87

Chapter 12  Lexicons . . . . . . . . . . . . . . . . . . . . . . . . . . . . . . . . . 91

Chapter 13  Concordances . . . . . . . . . . . . . . . . . . . . . . . . . . . . . 97

Chapter 14  Synopses . . . . . . . . . . . . . . . . . . . . . . . . . . . . . . . . 105

Chapter 15  Software Programs . . . . . . . . . . . . . . . . . . . . . . . . . 109

Chapter 16  Libraries: Their Nature and Use . . . . . . . . . . . . . . . . 117

Index: Authors/Editors/Compilers . . . . . . . . . . . . . . . . . 135

# Preface

The idea for this volume arose while I was engaged in graduate work at Southern Seminary. Struggling to identify and locate the literature I needed, I was fortunate to encounter a knowledgeable and helpful research librarian. There seemed to be no source with which he was not familiar. His familiarity with the several central research tools and reference guides saved me countless days and weeks of precious time.

Being in graduate school in the mid-sixties, I became aware of the various abstracting and indexing supports that were beginning to blossom. It was difficult to imagine someone actually doing "all that work" to prepare such helpful devices. Most of all, I was amazed to discover that vast amounts of time could be saved if one just knew how to utilize these valuable resources.

Today, graduate students at most institutions are required to take courses in library usage. There are many general guides that explore the labyrinth of theological research in general and the various tools and reference works that help simplify the task. Many large theological libraries have developed their own printed guides that acquaint the student with "helps" that save time and effort, always leaving more time for the central tasks of gathering, digesting, and collating information.

Today, on-line computer searches make enormous collections of data easier to manage. The problems of research have moved past the difficulties of gathering information and are now becoming focused on analyzing the vast amounts of data available. Of course, accompanying the information explosion has been a spate of books and essays that try to help scholars manage information by showing us how to make sense of it all.

In light of all that has been written to help researchers save time and focus their efforts, the question arises: "Why this book?" I believe that what I have tried to do here is not done in any other place—at least not as I conceive the task. My goal is to identify and describe briefly the resources that are available for NT research. Of course only a small portion of the research being carried out in the field is done in NT studies; therefore, many researchers will not find this volume particularly germane to their work. Further, because NT research is so pivotal to the other fields related to the study of the Christian faith (it often sets the agenda in related areas of research), a work such as this does have value outside the specific area of NT study.

Of course, a book with the breadth proposed in this one will contain a level of expertise that no single scholar could ever achieve. I know there will be "key" works that I have failed to cite; some works cited may, in fact, be marginal and not central to the subject under discussion. Even so, I hope there will be sufficient reference in any area to launch the inquisitive student in the right direction.

The large number of new books makes closing the "canon" here very difficult and imprecise. Between submission of this manuscript and publication of this book other works of signal importance will have appeared which could not be included here. It is the nature of a work such as this that it will become dated even before publication; nevertheless, there should be here a trail that will guide the student helpfully.

Furthermore, I have attempted to include some data in the several appendices that will prove helpful to researchers in the field of NT study. The list of publishers with addresses, for instance, is probably not usual fare for a book such as this, but helpful nonetheless.

I wish to thank Ms. Irene H. Palmer who faithfully typed and corrected the many drafts of this document. She has helped in many ways to improve this volume. The library staffs at Mercer University and Emory University have helped in numerous ways with my developing reference data. Finally, I wish to thank my good friend and colleague George Wesley Buchanan who read the final draft of this manuscript and offered many helpful suggestions for its improvement.

*Watson E. Mills*
*Mercer University*
*June 1995*

# CRITICAL TOOLS FOR THE STUDY OF THE NEW TESTAMENT

# CHAPTER 1

# Abbreviations

Unfortunately, abbreviations are not always consistent throughout the field of NT studies. Tables of commonly used abbreviations may be found in many biblical studies periodicals: cf. *JBL* (**3-024**); *CBQ* (**3-016**). The most comprehensive, single list of abbreviations for periodicals is Siegfried M. Schwertner, *Internationales Abkürzungsverzeichnis für Theologie und Grenzgebiete* (2nd ed. New York: de Gruyter, 1992). This mammoth volume provides rationale intended as the basis for a uniform system of abbreviations. The volume first lists abbreviations alphabetically, then provides the full names of the publications listed alphabetically. This latter section gives dates and places of publication as well as changes in the name of the journal, if any. It also indicates the volume numbers with reference to specific years.

The abbreviations supplied here take into account the lists mentioned above and attempts to follow them where possible; but, the shortest *unique* abbreviation is preferred.

# Journals

| | |
|---|---|
| ABR | *Australian Biblical Review* (Melbourne) |
| AfTJ | *Africa Theological Journal* (Tanzania, E. Africa) |
| AJP | *American Journal of Philology* (Baltimore, MD) |
| AJT | *American Journal of Theology* (Raleigh, NC) |
| AmER | *American Ecclesiastical Review* (Washington, DC) |
| AmiC | *L'Ami du Clergé* (Langres) |
| Ant | *Antonianum* (Rome) |
| ARefG | *Archiv für Reformationsgeschichte* (Gütersloh) |
| ASB | *Austin Seminary Bulletin* (Austin, TX) |
| AsSeign | *Assemblée du Seigneur* (Paris) |
| ATR | *Anglican Theological Review* (Evanston, IL) |
| AugM | *Augustinus* (Madrid) |
| AUSS | *Andrews University Seminary Studies* (Berrien Springs, MI) |
| B | *Biblica* (Rome) |
| BA | *Biblical Archaeologist* (Ann Arbor, MI) |
| BAR | *Biblical Archaeology Review* (Washington, DC) |
| BBC | *Bulletin of the Bezan Club* (Leiden) |
| Bes | *Bessarione, pubblicazione periodica di studi orientali* (Rome) |
| BI | *Biblical Interpretation* (Leiden) |
| BibL | *Bibel und Leben* (Düsseldorf) |
| BibN | *Biblische Notizen: Beiträge zur exegetischen Diskussion* (Bamberg, Germany) |
| BibO | *Bibbia e Oriente* (Brescia) |
| BibRev | *Bible Review* (Washington, DC) |
| BibT | *The Bible Translator* (Aberdeen, UK) |
| BibTo | *Bible Today* (Collegeville, MN) |
| Bij | *Bijdragen, Filosofie en Theologie* (Nijmegen) |
| BJRL | *Bulletin of the John Rylands Library* (Manchester, UK) After 1972, *Bulletin of the John Rylands University Library* |
| BK | *Bibel und Kirche* (Stuggart) |
| BL | *Bibel und Liturgie* (Vienna) |
| BLE | *Bulletin de littérature ecclésiastique* (Paris) |
| BQ | *Baptist Quarterly* (London) |
| BR | *Biblical Review* (New York) |

| | |
|---|---|
| BRel | *Books and Religion* (Durham, NC) |
| BRes | *Biblical Research* (Chicago) |
| BS | *Bibliotheca Sacra* (Dallas, TX) |
| BT | *Biblical Theology* (Belfast) |
| BTB | *Biblical Theology Bulletin* (Loudonville, NY) |
| BTS | *Bible et Terre Sainte* (Paris) |
| BTZ | *Berliner Theologische Zeitschrift* (Berlin) |
| Bur | *Burgense* (Burgos) |
| BVC | *Bible et vie Chrétienne* (Paris) |
| BView | *Biblical Viewpoint* (Greenville, SC) |
| BW | *Biblical World* (Chicago, IL) |
| BZ | *Biblische Zeitschrift* (Paderborn, Germany) |
| CalTJ | *Calvin Theological Journal* (Grand Rapids, MI) |
| Cath | *Catholica* (Münster) |
| CBG | *Collationes Brugenses et Gandavenses* (Gent) |
| CBQ | *Catholic Biblical Quarterly* (Washington, DC) |
| CBTJ | *Calvary Baptist Theological Journal* (Lansdale, PA) |
| CC | *Christian Century* (Chicago, IL) |
| CE | *Cahiers Évangiles* (Paris) |
| Ch | *Churchman* (St. Petersburg, FL) |
| ChH | *Church History* (Berne, IN) |
| CICR | *Communico: International Catholic Review* (Spokane, WA) |
| CJ | *Concordia Journal* (St. Louis, MO) |
| CJRT | *Canadian Journal of Religious Thought* (Toronto) |
| CJT | *Canadian Journal of Theology* (Toronto) |
| ClerR | *Clergy Review* (London) |
| CM | *Clergy Monthly* (Ranchi) |
| Coll | *Colloquium: The Australian and New Zealand Theological Society* (Adelaide) |
| Conci | *Concilium* (Rome) |
| CQ | *Crozer Quarterly* (Chester, PA) |
| CQR | *Church Quarterly Review* (London) |
| Crux | *Crux* (Vancouver) |
| CS | *Chicago Studies* (Mundelein, IL) |
| CSR | *Christian Scholars Review* (Grand Rapids, MI) |
| CT | *Christianity Today* (Chicago, IL) |

| | |
|---|---|
| CThM | *Currents in Theology and Mission* (St. Louis, MO) |
| CTM | *Concordia Theological Monthly* (St. Louis, MO) |
| CultB | *Cultura Bíblica* (Madrid) |
| DBM | *Deltío Biblikôn Meletôn* (Athens) |
| Dia | *Dialog* (Minneapolis, MN) |
| Did | *Didaskalia* (Lisbon) |
| Dir | *Direction: A Quarterly Publication of Mennonite Brethren Schools* (Fresno, CA) |
| Divinitas | *Divinitas* (Rome) |
| DR | *Downside Review* (Bath, UK) |
| DS | *Dominican Studies* (Oxford) |
| DTD | *Disciples Theological Digest* (St. Louis, MO) |
| DTT | *Dansk Teologisk Tidsskrift* (Copenhagen) |
| DunR | *Dunwoodie Review* (New York, NY) |
| E-I | *Eretz-Israel* (Jerusalem) |
| ED | *Euntes docete* (Rome) |
| EE | *Estudios eclesiásticos* (Madrid) |
| ÉgT | *Église et Théologie* (Ottawa) |
| EMQ | *Evangelical Mission Quarterly* (Wheaton, IL) |
| Enc | *Encounter* (Indianapolis, IN) |
| EphL | *Ephemerides liturgicae* (Rome) |
| EQ | *Evangelical Quarterly* (Exeter, UK) |
| Er | *Eranos, acta philologica suecana* (Gotoburgi) |
| EstBib | *Estudios bíblicos* (Madrid) |
| EstF | *Estudios Franciscanos* (Barcelona) |
| ET | *Expository Times* (Edinburgh, UK) |
| ETL | *Ephemerides Theologicae Lovaniensis* (Louvain) |
| ETR | *Études Théologiques et Religieuses* (Montpellier) |
| EV | *Esprit et Vie* (Langres) |
| EvErz | *Der evangelische Erzieher: Neue Folge der Zeitschriften: Haus und Kirche* (Frankfurt) |
| EvJ | *Evangelical Journal* (Myerstown, NJ) |
| EvT | *Evangelische Theologie* (Münich) |
| Exp | *The Expositor* (London) |
| FilN | *Filología Neotestamentaria* (Cordoba, Spain) |
| FM | *Faith and Mission* (Wake Forest, NC) |

| | |
|---|---|
| Forum | *Forum* (Sonoma, CA) |
| Found | *Foundations* (Herts, UK) |
| FV | *Foi et Vie* (Paris) |
| FZPT | *Freiburger Zeitschrift für Philsophie und Theologie* (Freiburg, Switzerland) |
| GeistL | *Geist und Leben* (Münich) |
| GOTR | *Greek Orthodox Theological Review* (Brookline, MA) |
| GR | *Gordon Review* (Boston) |
| Greg | *Gregorianum* (Rome) |
| GTJ | *Grace Theological Journal* (Winona Lake, IN) |
| GTT | *Gereformeered theologisch tijdschrift* (Heusden) |
| HartQ | *Hartford Quarterly* (Hartford, CT) |
| HBT | *Horizons in Biblical Theology: An International Dialogue* (Pittsburgh, PA) |
| Herm | *Hermathena* (Dublin) |
| HeyJ | *Heythrop Journal* (London) |
| HJ | *Hibbert Journal* (London) |
| HTR | *Harvard Theological Review* (Cambridge, MA) |
| HTS | *Hervormde Teologiese Studies* (Pretoria, South Africa) |
| IBS | *Irish Biblical Studies* (Belfast, N. Ireland) |
| IEJ | *Israel Exploration Journal* (Jerusalem) |
| IJT | *Indian Journal of Theology* (Serampore) |
| IKZ | *Internationale Kirchliche Zeitschrift* (Bern) |
| Interp | *Interpretation* (Richmond, VA) |
| IRM | *International Review of Mission* (Geneva, Switzerland) |
| ITQ | *Irish Theological Quarterly* (Maynooth, UK) |
| ITS | *Indian Theological Studies* (Bangalore) |
| JAAR | *Journal of the American Academy of Religion* (Atlanta, GA) |
| JASA | *Journal of the American Scientific Affiliation* (Ipswich, MA) |
| JBL | *Journal of Biblical Literature* (Atlanta, GA) |
| JBR | *Journal of Bible and Religion* (Brattleboro, VT) |
| JCE | *Journal of Christian Education* (Sydney, Australia) |
| JCSP | *Journal of Classical and Sacred Philology* (Cambridge, UK) |
| JEH | *Journal of Ecclesiastical History* (London) |
| JES | *Journal of Ecumenical Studies* (Valley Forge, PA) |
| JETS | *Journal of the Evangelical Theological Society* (Wheaton, IL) |

| | |
|---|---|
| JJS | *Journal of Jewish Studies* (Oxford, UK) |
| JLR | *Journal of Law and Religion* (St. Paul, MN) |
| JNES | *Journal of Near Eastern Studies* (Chicago, IL) |
| JPH | *Journal of Presbyterian History* (Philadelphia, PA) |
| JQR | *Jewish Quarterly Review* (Leiden) |
| JR | *Journal of Religion* (Chicago, IL) |
| JRE | *Journal of Religious Ethics* (Atlanta, GA) |
| JRT | *Journal of Religious Thought* (Washington, DC) |
| JRTI | *Journal of Religious and Theological Information* (Binghamton NY) |
| JSNT | *Journal for the Study of the New Testament* (Sheffield, UK) |
| JSOT | *Journal for the Study of the Old Testament* (Sheffield, UK) |
| JSS | *Journal of Semitic Studies* (Manchester, UK) |
| JTS | *Journal of Theological Studies* (Oxford, UK) |
| JTSA | *Journal of Theology for Southern Africa* (Capetown, South Africa) |
| K | *Kairos: Zeitschrift für Religionswissenschaft und Theologie* (Salzburg, Austria) |
| KD | *Kerygma und Dogma, Zeitschrift für theologische Forschung und kirchliche Lehre* (Göttingen) |
| KRS | *Kirchenblatt für die Reformierte Schweiz* (Basel, Switzerland) |
| Lat | *Lateranum* (Rome) |
| LB | *Linguistica Biblica* (Bonn, Germany) |
| LCQ | *Lutheran Church Quarterly* (Gettysburg, PA) |
| LCR | *Lutheran Church Review* (Philadelphia, PA) |
| Levant | *Levant: Journal of the British School of Archaeology in Jerusalem* (London) |
| LexTQ | *Lexington Theological Quarterly* (Lexington, KY) |
| LouvS | *Louvain Studies* (Louvain) |
| LPT | *Laval Théologique et Philosophique* (Laval, Quebec, Canada) |
| LQ | *Lutheran Quarterly* (St. Paul, MN) |
| LQHR | *London Quarterly and Holbon Review* (London) |
| LTJ | *Lutheran Theological Journal* (Adelaide, Australia) |
| Luth | *Luthertum* (Erlangen, Germany) formerly *Neue kirchliche Zeitschrift* |
| LuthW | *Lutheran World* (Geneva) |
| LV | *Lumen Vitae* (Brussels) |

| LVie | *Lumière et Vie* (Lyons, France) |
| MD | *Maison-Dieu: Revue de Pastorale Liturgique* (Paris) |
| MeliT | *Melita Theologica* (Rabat, Malta) |
| Miss | *Missiology: An International Review* (Scottdale, PA) |
| Missionalia | *Missionalia* (Pretoria, S. Africa) |
| Mn | *Mnemosyne, bibliotheca classica batava* (Leiden) |
| MQR | *Mennonite Quarterly Review* (Goshen, IN) |
| MSR | *Mélanges de Science Religieuse* (Lille, France) |
| MTZ | *Münchener theologische Zeitschrift* (München) |
| NBlack | *New Blackfriars* (London) |
| NedTT | *Nederlands theologisch tijdschrift* (Wageningen) |
| Neo | *Neotestamentica* (Pretoria) |
| NKZ | *Neue kirchliche Zeitschrift* (Erlangen) See *Luthertum* |
| NRT | *La Nouvelle revue théologique* (Louvain) |
| NovT | *Novum Testamentum* (Leiden) |
| NTheoR | *New Theology Review* (Wilmington, DE) |
| NTS | *Nieuwe theologische studiën* (Wageningen) |
| NTSt | *New Testament Studies* (Cambridge, NY) |
| NTT | *Norsk teologisk tidsskrift* (Oslo) |
| Num | *Numen* (International Association for the History of Religions) (Leiden) |
| Nunt | *Nuntius sodalicii neotestamentici Upsaliensis* (Lund) |
| NZSTR | *Neue Zeitschrift für systematische Theologie und Religions-philosophie* (Berlin) |
| O | *Orpheus: revista di umanità classica e cristiana* (Catania) |
| OC | *Oriens christianus* (Wiesbaden) |
| OCP | *Orientalia christiana periodica* (Rome) |
| OrBibLov | *Orientalia et Biblica Louvaniensa* (Louvain) |
| OS | *L'orient syrien* (Paris) |
| Para | *Paraclete* (Springfield, MO) |
| ParaM | *Parabola Magazine* (New York) |
| PATS | *Pacifica: Australian Theological Studies* (Brunswick, Australia) |
| PB | *Przegląd biblijny* (Warsaw) |
| PJ | *Perkins Journal* (Dallas, TX) |
| Prot | *Protestantesimo* (Rome) |
| PRS | *Perspectives in Religious Studies* (Macon, GA) |

| | |
|---|---|
| PSB | *Princeton Seminary Bulletin* (Princeton, NJ) |
| PTR | *Princeton Theological Review* (Princeton, NJ) |
| Qad | *Qadmoniot* (Jerusalem) |
| QR | *Quarterly Review* (Nashville, TN) |
| RAfT | *Revue Africaine de Théologie* (Alger) |
| RB | *Revue biblique* (Paris) |
| RBén | *Revue Bénédictine* (Maredsous) |
| RE | *Review and Expositor* (Louisville, KY) |
| REd | *Religious Education* (New Haven, CT) |
| Reformatio | *Reformatio: Zeitschrift für evangelische Kultur und Politik* (Zürich) |
| RefR | *Reformed Review* (New Brunswick, NJ) |
| RelSR | *Religious Studies Review* (Valpariso, IN) |
| RET | *Revista española de teología* (Madrid) |
| RevAug | *Revista Augstiniana de espiritualidad* (Calahorra) |
| RevB | *Revista Bíblica* (Buenos Aires) |
| RevQ | *Revue de Qumran* (Paris) |
| RevSR | *Revue des Sciences Religieuses* (Strasbourg) |
| RHLR | *Revue d'historie et de littérature religieuses* (Paris) |
| RHPR | *Revue d'historie et de philosophie religieuses* (Strasbourg) |
| RHR | *Revue de l'historie des religions* (Paris) |
| RivB | *Rivista Biblica* (Bologna) |
| RL | *Religion in Life* (New York) |
| RMAL | *Revue du moyen âge latin* (Strasbourg) |
| ROC | *Revue de l'orient chrétien* (Paris) |
| RoczTK | *Roczniki Teologiczno-Kanoniczne* (Lublin) |
| RQ | *Restoration Quarterly* (Abilene, TX) |
| RR | *Richerche religiose* (Rome) |
| RSPT | *Revue des Sciences Philosophiques et Thélogiques* (Paris) |
| RSR | *Recherches de science religieuse* (Paris) (= *SR*, 1943-1943) |
| RT | *Revue Thomiste* (Paris) |
| RTAM | *Recherches de Théologie Ancienne et Médiévale* (Louvain) |
| RTR | *Reformed Theological Review* (Hawthorn, Australia) |
| RW | *Reformed World* (Geneva) |
| SacD | *Sacra Docttrina* (Bologna) |
| Sale | *Salesianum* (Rome) |

| | |
|---|---|
| Salm | *Salmanticensis* (Salamanca) |
| SBib | *Sémiotique et Bible* (Lyon Cedex) |
| SBLSP | *Society of Biblical Literature Seminar Papers* (Atlanta, GA) |
| ScE | *Science et Esprit* (Burges) |
| Scr | *Scripture* (Edinburg) Later *Scripture Bulletin* |
| ScrB | *Scripture Bulletin* (Edinburgh) |
| ScripT | *Scripta theologica* (Pamplona) |
| ScrSA | *Scriptura: Journal of Bible and Theology in Southern Africa* (Stellenbosch, South Africa) |
| SE | *Sciences Ecclésiastiques* (Montréal) |
| SEAJT | *South East Asia Journal of Theology* (Singapore) |
| SEc | *Studi Ecumenici* (Verno) |
| SecC | *Second Century* (Malibu, CA) |
| Semeia | *Semeia* (Atlanta) |
| SJT | *Scottish Journal of Theology* (Edinburgh, UK) |
| SLJT | *Saint Luke's Journal of Theology* (Sewanee, TN) |
| SM | *Studia Missionalia* (Rome) |
| SNTU-A | *Studien zum NT und seiner Umwelt* (Linz) |
| SO | *Symbolae osloenses* (Oslo) |
| SouJT | *Southwestern Journal of Theology* (Fort Worth, TX) |
| Soundings | *Soundings* (Nashville, TN) |
| SR | *Science religieuse, travaux et recherches* (Paris) |
| SRel | *Studies in Religion/Sciences religieuses* (Toronto) |
| ST | *Studia Theologica* (Oslo) |
| STK | *Svensk teologisk kvartalskrift* (Lund) |
| STZ | *Theologische Zeitschrift aus der Schweiz.* After 1900, *Schweizerische theologische Zeitschrift* (Zürich) |
| SuC | *La Suola Cattolica* (Milan) |
| SVTQ | *Saint Vladimir's Theological Quarterly* (New York) |
| TB | *Theologische Blätter* (Leipzig) |
| TBe | *Theologische Beiträge* (Harr, Germany) |
| TD | *Theology Digest* (St. Mary, KS) |
| TEd | *Theological Educator* (New Orleans, LA) |
| TGl | *Theologie und Glaube* (Paderborn, Germany) |
| Th | *Theology* (London) |
| Themelios | *Themelios* (London) |

| Thomist | *Thomist* (Washington, DC) |
|---|---|
| ThPh | *Theologie und Philosophie* (Freiburg, Germany) |
| ThSt | *Theological Studies* (Washington, DC) |
| TLZ | *Theologische Literaturzeitung* (Leipzig) |
| TQ | *Theologische Quartalschrift* (Freiburg) |
| TR | *Theologische Rundschau* (Tübingen) |
| Trans | *Transformation* (Fort Lee, NJ) |
| TriJ | *Trinity Journal* (Deerfield, IL) |
| TS | *Theologische Studiën* (Utrecht) |
| TSFB | *Theological Students' Fellowship Bulletin* (Madison, WI) |
| TSK | *Theologische Studien und Kritiken* (Gotha) |
| TSR | *Trinity Seminary Review* (Columbus, OH) |
| TsT | *Tijdschrift voor Theologie* (Nijmegen) |
| TT | *Theologische Tijdschrift* (Leiden) |
| TTod | *Theology Today* (Princeton, NJ) |
| TTZ | *Trierer Theologische Zeitschrift* (Trierer) |
| TXav | *Theologica Xaveriana* (Bogata, Colombia) |
| TxK | *Texte und Kontexte* (Stuttgart, Germany) |
| TynB | *Tyndale Bulletin* (Chicago, IL) |
| TZ | *Theologische Zeitschrift* (Basel) |
| USQR | *Union Seminary Quarterly Review* (New York, NY) |
| USR | *Union Seminary Review* (Hampden-Sydney, VA) |
| VC | *Vigiliae Christianae* (Leiden) |
| VD | *Verbum Domini* (Rome) |
| VoxEv | *Vox Evangelica* (London) |
| VP | *Vivre et Penser* (Paris) |
| VS | *La Vie Spirituelle* (Paris) |
| VT | *Vetus Testamentum* (Leiden) |
| WoD | *Word und Dienst* (Bethel) |
| Worship | *Worship* (Collegeville, MN) |
| WTJ | *Westminster Theological Journal* (Philadelphia, PA) |
| WuW | *Wissenschaft und Weisheit* (Münich/Gladbach) |
| WW | *Word & World* (St. Paul, MN) |
| ŽA | *Živa Antika* (Skoplje) |
| ZAW | *Zeitschrift für die alttestamentliche Wissenschaft* (Berlin) |
| ZEE | *Zeitschrift für Evangelische Ethik* (Gütersloh) |

| | |
|---|---|
| Zion | *Zion* (Jerusalem) |
| ZKG | *Zeitschrift für Kirchengeschichte* (Stuttgart, Germany) |
| ZKT | *Zeitschrift für Katholische Theologie* (Innsbruck) |
| ZNW | *Zeitschrift für die neutestamentliche Wissenschaft und die Kunde der älteren Kirche* (Berlin) |
| ZRGG | *Zeitschrift für Religions- und Geistesgeschichte* (Köln) |
| ZST | *Zeitschrift für systematische Theologie* (Berlin) |
| ZTK | *Zeitschrift für Theologie und Kirche* (Tübingen) |
| ZWT | *Zeitschrift für wissenschaftliche Theologie* (Leipzig) |
| ZWTh | *Zeitschrift für wissenschaftliche Theologie* (Scultzbach, 1827-1828) |

# Series

| | |
|---|---|
| AAOS | *Annual of the American Schools of Oriental Research* |
| ALBO | *Analecta lovaniensia biblica et orientalia* |
| AnBib | *Analecta biblica* |
| ANTF | *Arbeiten zur neutestamentlichen Textforschung* |
| ASNU | *Acta seminarii neotestamentici upsaliensis* |
| ASTI | *Annual of the Swedish Theological Institute* |
| ATANT | *Abhandlungen zur Theologie des Alten und Neuen Testaments* |
| BBB | *Bonner biblische Beiträge* |
| BibB | *Biblische Beiträge* |
| BibOr | *Biblica et orientalia* |
| BWANT | *Beiträge zur Wissenschaft vom Alten und Neuen Testament* |
| CahT | *Cahiers théologiques* |
| CBQMS | *Catholic Biblical Quarterly Monograph Series* |
| ConB | *Coniectanea biblica* |
| ConN | *Coniectanea neotestamentia* |
| ExA | *Ex Auditu: An Annual of the Frederick Neumann Symposium on Theological Interpretation of Scripture* |
| FRLANT | *Forschungen zur Religion und Literatur des Alten und Neuen Testaments* |
| GCAJS | *Gratz College Annual of Jewish Studies* |
| GNT | *Grundrisse zum Neuen Testament* |
| HDR | *Harvard Dissertations in Religion* |
| HTS | *Harvard Theological Studies* |
| HUCA | *Hebrew Union College Annual* |
| JSNTSup | *Journal for the Study of the New Testament: Supplement Series* |
| NovTSup | *Novum Testamentum Supplement* |
| NTAbh | *Neutestamentliche Abhandlungen* |
| NTF | *Neutestamentliche Forschung* |
| NTTS | *New Testament Tools and Studies* |
| PSBA | *Proceedings of the Society of Biblical Archaeology* |
| SANT | *Studien zum Alten und Neuen Testament* |
| SB | *Sources bibliques* |
| SBB | *Stuttgarter biblische Beiträge* |
| SBFLA | *Studii Biblici Franciscani Liber Annuus* |
| SBLASP | *Society of Biblical Literature Abstracts and Seminar Papers* |

| | |
|---|---|
| SBLDS | *Society of Biblical Literature Dissertation Series* |
| SBLMS | *Society of Biblical Literature Monograph Series* |
| SBLSBS | *Society of Biblical Literature Sources for Biblical Study* |
| SBLTT | *Society of Biblical Literature Texts and Translations* |
| SBM | *Stuttgarter biblische Monographien* |
| SBS | *Stuttgarter Bibelstudien* |
| SBT | *Studies in Biblical Theology* |
| SCHNT | *Studia ad corpus hellenisticum Novi Testamenti* |
| SEÅ | *Svensk Exegetisk Årsbok* |
| SNT | *Studien zum Neuen Testament* |
| SNTSMS | *Society for New Testament Studies Monograph Series* |
| SUNT | *Studien zur Umwelt des Neuen Testament* |
| TU | *Texte und Untersuchungen* |
| UNT | *Untersuchungen zum Neuen Testament* |
| WMANT | *Wissenschaftliche Monographien zum Alten und Neuen Testament* |

## Reference Works

| | |
|---|---|
| AG | Arndt, W. F., F. W. Gingrich, and F. W. Danker (eds.). *A Greek-English Lexicon of the New Testament and Other Early Christian Literature* |
| ANEP | Pritchard, J. B. *The Ancient Near East in Pictures Relating to the Old Testament* |
| BETL | *Bibliotheca Ephemeridum Theologicarum Lovaniensium* |
| BNTC | *Black's New Testament Commentaries* |
| CaB | *Cambridge Bible for Schools and Colleges* |
| CGTC | *Cambridge Greek Testament Commentary* |
| CNT | *Commentaire du Nouveau Testament* |
| DBS | Cazelles, H. (ed.). *Dictionnaire de la Bible, Supplément* |
| HNT | *Handbuch zum Neuen Testament* |
| HSNTA | Hennecke-Schneemelcher. *New Testament Apocrypha* |
| HThK | *Herders Theologischer Kommentar zum Neuen Testament* |
| IB | *Interpreter's Bible* |
| ICC | *International Critical Commentary* |
| IDB | *Interpreter's Dictionary of the Bible* |
| LCL | Loeb Classical Library |
| LS | Lindell, H. G. and R. Scott. *A Greek-English Lexicon* |
| KEK | Kritisch-exegetischer Kommentar über das Neue Testament |
| JANT | James, M. R. *The Apocryphal New Testament* |
| M-M | Moulton-Milligan. *Vocabulary of the Greek Testament* |
| NICNT | *New International Commentary on the New Testament* |
| OABA | *Oxford Annotated Bible with the Apocrypha* |
| PNTC | *Pelican New Testament Commentary* |
| TBC | *Torch Bible Commentaries* |
| TDNT | Kittel, K. and G. W. Bromiley (eds.). *Theological Dictionary of the New Testament* |

# CHAPTER 2

# Bibliographies

In the simplest terms, a bibliography is a well-ordered collection of books and other writings relating to a specific area of research. Usually, a bibliography attempts to include citations to the various systems of interpretation and methods of approach by including materials reflecting these different schools of thought as these relate to a specific research topic.

Before Gutenberg, the term "bibliography" referred to the process whereby a book was copied, i.e., reproduced by a scribe or copyist.[1] It was not until the eighteenth century that the term came into common usage. It then referred to the writing *about* books instead of the writing *of* books. Specifically,

---

[1] The term "bibliography" was first used in anything approaching its modern sense in 1763 by Du Bure (*Bibliographie Instructiv*).

it then described the process of copying the title page and colophon of a given book so that this information could be catalogued and identified by later researchers to assist them in identifying and locating materials.

Later, in the nineteenth century, bibliographies set out to produce lists of all the books ever published. As the number of published books grew exponentially, efforts were no longer taken to be definitive, and today, most bibliographies are lists of information (e.g., books, articles, etc.), that relate to specific research areas. Theodore Bestermann defined a bibliography as "a list of books arranged according to some permanent principle."[2]

Modern bibliographies are intended to direct the reader (1) to the most significant reference works in a specific research area and (2) to the "standard" or "classic" works in that area. Bibliographies may be selective (i.e., limit themselves to certain kinds of materials that are indispensable to a specific research area) or comprehensive (i.e., attempt to cover as completely as possible the area delineated by listing all relevant materials). In fact, most bibliographies fall in between these two types. Frequently, entries in a given bibliography are annotated with information other than the actual citation. This data describes the particular item indicating its structure, inclusiveness, general usefulness, strengths and weaknesses, etc.

Bibliographical collections usually fall into two distinct categories: (1) classified bibliographies and (2) chronological bibliographies.

Classified bibliographies provide wide coverage of material that is judged to be the best of previous scholarship in a given research area. Obviously, such

---

[2]Theodore Bestermann, *A World Bibliography of Bibliographies and Bibliographical Catalogues, Calendars, Abstracts, Digests, Indexes and the Like* (4th ed. rev.; Lausanne: Societas Bibliographica, 1965), I: 17 (**2-001**).

bibliographies are necessarily selective, ignoring those works that have failed to withstand the critical evaluations of researchers.

Chronological bibliographies pull together the works in a given research area during a specified period of time. These often lack perspective though they tend to be more comprehensive than do the classified bibliographies.

In dissertation research, students are usually expected to utilize both types of bibliographies. This chapter will identify some of the major bibliographies available for NT study. For a more detailed listing of bibliographies see Hurd, *A Bibliography of New Testament Bibliographies* (**2-007**).

## Bibliographies of Bibliographies

### General Bibliographies

**2-001**      Bestermann, Theodore. *A World Bibliography of Bibliographies and of Bibliographical Catalogues, Calendars, Abstracts, Digests, Indexes and the Like*. 5 vols. Lausanne: Societas Bibliographica, 1965-1966. The volume lists over 117,000 separately published bibliographies arranged under 16,000 subject headings which appear in alphabetical order. The five volumes cover bibliographies published through 1963; the work has been updated by Toomey (**2-005**). Volume five contains an author index.

**2-002**      *Bibliographic Index: A Cumulative Bibliography of Bibliographies, 1937-*. Wilson Company, 1938. This work cites bibliographies that are published separately as well as those appearing in books, journals, festschriften, etc. The Index reports on bibliographies that have been published in approximately 2,000 foreign and English language periodicals. The arrangement is by subject headings and lists bibliographies that contain 50 or more citations.

**2-003**      Collison, Robert L. *Bibliographies, Subject and National: A Guide to Their Contents, Arrangement, and Use*. 3rd ed.

Lockwood Press, 1968. A good basic guide to major bibliographies in any specific field. Includes references to major works that contain bibliographies.

2-004     Gray, Richard A. *Serial Bibliographies in the Humanities and the Social Sciences*. Pierian Books, 1969. Contains references to ongoing bibliographies including those that appear as a part of scholarly journals. Includes indices by title, author, publisher, and subject.

2-005     Toomey, Alice F. *A World Bibliography of Bibliographies 1964-1974*. 2 vols. Rowman & Littlefield, 1977. This work is a continuation of **2-001** though its nature and scope is somewhat more limited than in Bestermann. The work is actually a reproduction of more than 18,000 LC printed cards arranged under approximately 6,000 subheadings.

## Biblical Studies Bibliographies

2-006     Barrow, John G. *A Bibliography of Bibliographies in Religion*. Edwards, 1955. Lists separately published bibliographies from the fifteenth century through 1952. The entries are arranged by subject and then chronologically within the subject area. The work contains an author index. The entries are annotated. There is a "location" code indicating where the book may be found. This volume remains the standard bibliographic guide.

2-007     Hurd, John C., Jr. *A Bibliography of New Testament Bibliographies*. Seabury, 1966. This important work lists, in systematic fashion, bibliographies on books of the NT, specific NT words, methods of study, etc. The bibliographies listed range from those appended to elementary college introductory texts to comprehensive research bibliographies. The work also includes a section that indicates where a student may find these bibliographies. This is an excellent resource that must be consulted by any serious student.

2-008     Shunami, Shlomo. *Bibliography of Jewish Bibliographies*. Magnes, 1969. This work includes references to more than 4,700 bibliographies concerning Jewish literature, ancient Israel, and the various books of the Bible.

2-009    Smith, Wilbur M. *A List of Bibliographies of Theological and Biblical Literature Published in Great Britain and America, 1595-1932: with Critical, Biographical, and Bibliographical Notes.* Privately published, 1931. This work includes brief annotations as well as biographical information on the author of each bibliography. The entries are arranged by date and not by subject; thus, its usefulness is limited to the student's diligence.

## General Reference Bibliographies

2-010    *ADRIS Newsletter: Newsletter of the Association for the Development of Religious Information Systems.* Bronx, NY: Department of Theology at Fordham University, 1971- . This relatively new publication has already established itself as a leader in this emerging field. The publication contains a wealth of information including news, announcements, bibliography, new research, announcements of new and established periodicals, as well as selected reviews.

2-011    *Aids to a Theological Library: Selected Basic Reference Books and Periodicals.* American Association of Theological Schools, 1969. Although this work is intended primarily for use by acquisitions librarians, the work is also useful in assisting students in identifying basic tools necessary for research in most theological areas. This 95 page work lists basic theological reference tools and bibliographies. Without annotation.

2-012    *American Book Publishing Record.* Bowker Company, 1960- . This monthly publication consists of the information that appears in *Publisher's Weekly.* The entries are arranged according to Dewey. There is an annual cumulation that consolidates the monthly listing by subject and provides complete author/subject indices as well.

2-013    *American Reference Books Annual.* Libraries Unlimited, 1970- . This annual volume covers reference books published or re-published in America in the previous year. There are ample indices. The arrangement is classified by topics. Each entry includes full bibliographical data as well as descriptive and evaluative notes.

2-014       *Arts and Humanities Index.* Philadelphia: Institute for Scientific
            Information, 1978- . Published three times annually, this
            index is arranged in two parts: the first section includes
            journal lists, subject index, and citation index; the second
            section includes a source and corporate index. The work
            covers more than 1,000 periodicals, mostly English
            language publications. It provides a detailed list of materials
            that are useful in many areas that are related to biblical and
            theological studies.

2-015       Baer, Eleanora A. (comp.). *Titles in Series: A Handbook for
            Librarians and Students.* 3rd ed., 4 vols. Scarecrow Press,
            1978. This work contains approximately 70,000 titles
            published in series (up to 1975). The first two volumes list
            the titles by series while volumes three and four contain an
            author and title index as well as a series index. There is
            also a directory of publishers.

2-016       *Books in Print: An Author-Title-Series Index to "Publishers Trade
            List Annual."* Bowker Company, 1948- . An annual
            publication that provides a very useful arrangement of the
            information contained in the *Publisher's Trade List Annual*
            (also published by Bowker). Each annual volume lists over
            500,000 titles that are available from more than 4,000
            American publishers.

2-017       *Books in Series in the United States, 1966-1975: Original,
            Reprinted, In-Print and Out-of-Print Books Published or
            Distributed in the U.S. in Popular, Scholarly and
            Professional Series.* Bowker Company, 1977. This guide
            lists more than 86,000 books from some 9,300 different
            series published by over 1,000 different publishers. Indices
            include author, title, and subject. A supplement entitled
            *Books in Series in the United States, 1966-1975: Original,
            Reprinted, In-Print and Out-of-Print Books Published or
            Distributed in the U.S. in Popular Scholarly and
            Professional Series: Supplement* is arranged in the same
            way and lists an additional 10,700 titles. For books in series
            before 1966, see **2-015**.

2-018       *Critical Guide to Catholic Reference Works.* 2nd ed. Libraries
            Unlimited, 1980. This annotated bibliography refers to more
            than 1,000 reference books on Roman Catholicism. It
            covers all aspects of Roman Catholic thought, teaching,
            theology, history, and practice. The evaluative annotations

provide numerous cross-references to other works of interest. There is a comprehensive index that includes author, title, and subject entries.

2-019 *Reference Works for Theological Research: An Annotated Selective Bibliographical Guide.* Westminster Theological Seminary, 1986. These 283 pages are arranged into two main sections: general theological/religious lists (chapters on encyclopedias, dissertations, periodicals, various writing and research tools), and subject area lists (works that deal with biblical studies, church history, philosophy, etc.). The more than 800 entries which constitute the 39 chapters of the book are concisely annotated. There are detailed indices listing authors, editors, compilers, and titles. The work precedes *Reference Works for Theological Research: A Selected Bibliography* (Trinity Evangelical School, Rolfing Memorial Library, 1978).

2-020 *Religious Reading: The Annual Guide.* Consortium Books, 1971. The work undertakes to cite all publications in the area of religious studies from all American publishers each year. The entries are arranged by broad subject areas with specific subdivisions. Indices include author, title, and publisher.

2-021 Sayre, John Leslie, Jr. and Roberta Hamburger. *Tools for Theological Research.* 5th ed. Seminary Press, 1981. Designed for theological students, the annotations are carefully written for those who are unfamiliar with theological reference works and general research. The titles grow out of course work required at Philips University Graduate Seminary and focus on the general area of theological bibliography. See also Sayre, John Leslie, Jr. and Roberta Hamburger, *Theological Bibliography and Research.* Philips University Graduate Seminary, 1972.

2-022 *Theological Bibliographies: Essential Books for a Minister's Library.* The Andover Newton Quarterly. A guide that lists in a classified arrangement works chosen and annotated by the faculty of the Andover Newton Seminary. The works are chosen especially for Protestant clergy.

2-023 *Union List of Serials.* Chicago Area Theological Library Association, 1974. The Chicago Area Theological Library Association consists of 17 Protestant and 5 Roman Catholic libraries. A compilation that lists more than 6,000 serial titles that may be found in these libraries. Periodicals are listed alphabetically by titles.

2-024     Walsh, Michael J. (comp.). *Religious Bibliographies in Social Literature: A Guide.* Westport, CT: Greenwood Press, 1981. Describes some 175 current periodicals with specific reference to religious studies bibliographies. Alphabetical entries with full biographical data including publishers' addresses.

## General Biblical Bibliographies

2-025     Ackroyd, Peter R. (ed.). *Bible Bibliography, 1967-1973: Old Testament.* Blackwell, 1974. This volume contains annotation on approximately 1,900 titles in the fields of archaeology, exegesis, history, introductions, theology, Qumran, grammar, etc. Materials are arranged alphabetically under the various topics.

2-026     Aland, Kurt. *Kurzgefasste Liste der Griechischen Handschriften des Neuen Testaments.* Vol. 1. Walter de Gruyter und Kompagnie, 1963. The first volume of a series projected to consist of four volumes aiming at listing all known Greek papyri and manuscript fragments relating to the Greek NT. Each volume provides data concerning the manuscripts listed such as its description, location, and references to the numbering guides used to refer to these documents in standard Greek texts.

2-027     American Bible Society. *Scriptures of the World: A Compilation of 1603 Languages in Which at Least One Book of the Bible Has Been Published.* United Bible Societies, 1976. A work of 106 pages on which materials are listed in alphabetical order and in chronological order of first publication. The volume includes various maps.

2-028     Anderson, George W. (ed.). *A Decade of Bible Bibliography: The Book Lists of the Society for Old Testament Study, 1957-1966.* Basil Blackwell and Mott, 1967. This volume continues an earlier work done by Roley and contains approximately 1,500 entries. The entries are well annotated.

2-029     Armstrong, James F., et al. *A Bibliography of Bible Study for Theological Students.* 2nd ed., edited by Bruce Manning

Metzger. Princeton Seminary Pamphlets 1. Princeton Theological Seminary, 1960. First published in 1948, this work lists important English titles with a few foreign language texts and grammars. Without annotations.

2-030    *Bibliographie Biblique.* Les Facultés de Théologie et de Philosophie de la Compagnie de Jesus, 1958. Limited to Catholic periodicals and books in French, English, and Latin, this work contains more than 9,000 entries from the period 1920-1957. There is a detailed classification system. Serial coverage is limited to 29 Catholic titles.

2-031    *Book List of the Society for Old Testament Study.* Vol. 1- . Society for Old Testament Study, 1946- ; annual. The ten subject areas provide reviews of 400 items. Coverage is international and current. The work includes monographs, dictionaries, encyclopedias, festschriften, and conference proceedings. Each issue includes a list of books received and an author index.

2-032    Brock, Sebastien P., Charles J. Fritsch, and Sidney Jellicoe. *A Classified Bibliography of the Septuagint. Arbeiten aur Literatur und Geschichte des Hellenistischen Judentums,* Bd. 6. Brill, 1973. The volume provides bibliography on the Septuagint down to 1969. It also contains important reviews and an author index.

2-033    Buchard, Christoph. *Bibliographie zu den Handschriften vom Toten Meer.* 2 vols. Beihefte zur Zeitschrift für die Alttestamentliche Wissenschaft, Bd. 76, 89. Alfred Töpelmann, 1957-1965. Probably the most comprehensive bibliography on the Dead Sea Scrolls, this two-volume work contains references to more than 4,500 articles and books. Volume I covers up until 1955; Volume II covers 1956-1962.

2-034    Charlesworth, James Hamilton and P. Dykers. *The Pseudepigrapha and Modern Research.* Septuagint and Cognate Studies 7. Scholars Press for the Society of Biblical Literature, 1976. The 1,494 entries in this volume were written between 1960-1975. Included are articles, books, parts of books, monographs, and essays. The entries are not annotated, but there is a narrative introduction to each section that "frames" the current research.

2-035         Danker, F. W. *Multipurpose Tools for Bible Study.* 3rd ed.
Concordia Publishing House, 1970. The volume contains
chapters on concordances, the Nestle text, the Hebrew OT,
the history of the LXX, the use of the LXX, Hebrew OT
grammars and lexicons, Greek NT grammars and lexicons,
the use of grammars and lexicons, Bible dictionaries, Bible
versions, the use of English Bible versions, Judaica,
archaeology, the Dead Sea Scrolls, commentaries and their
uses. The amount of information contained in this brief
volume is unbelievable. Necessary for the serious
researcher. This is the most extensive guide available. It is
international in its scope.

2-036         Darlow, T. H. and H. F. Moule (comps.). *Historical Catalogue of
the Printed Editions of Holy Scripture in the Library of the
British and Foreign Bible Society.* 2 vols. in 4. London:
Bible House, 1903-1911. Reprint. 2 vols. in 4. Kraus
Reprint, 1968. These two volumes list over 100,000 editions
of the Bible. The arrangement is chronological by language.
There are brief annotations. Volume I covers English
language editions, and Volume II covers all other languages
as well as polyglot editions. Extensive indices are contained
in Volume II.

2-037         Delling, Gerhard (ed.). *Bibliographie zur Jüdisch-Hellenistischen
und Intertestamentarischen Literatur, 1900-1970. In
Verbindung mit Malwine Maser. Texte und Untersuchungen
zur geschichte der Altchristlichen Literatur,* Bd. 106.
Akademic Verlag, 1975. This bibliography has 39 sections
consisting of carefully selected works that deal with
Hellenistic Judaism and the life of the Jews during the
Diaspora. The work contains an author index.

2-038         *Ecole Biblique et Archéologique Française. Bibliothèque.*
Catalogue de la Bibliothèque de l'Ecole Biblique et
Archéologique Française/Catalog of the Library of the
French Biblical and Archaeological School. 13 vols. G. K.
Hall and Company, 1975. These 13 volumes contain
references to 215,000 articles and books covering
linguistics, Egyptology, Assyriology, archaeology, etc.
Journal articles are taken from more than 300 journals.

2-039         *Elenchus bibliographicus biblicus.* Rome: Biblical Institute 1968- .
An annual publication, this valuable index to biblical
literature and secondary material lists articles, books, and

reviews. It also notes when materials are reprinted in other collections and/or translations. Extremely important for definitive listings in any NT area of study. Covers all important journals in all languages. Issued originally as a part of *Biblica* (**3-010**), but separately since 1968. Arranged by subject, this comprehensive listing of books, articles, Hebrew and Greek words in the areas of the OT, NT, intertestamental Judaism and the early patristic period contains full index, list of abbreviations, table of contents.

**2-040** Erbacher, Hermann. *Bibliographie der Fest- und Gedenkschriften für Personlichkeiten aus Evangelischer Theologie und Kirche, 1881-1969. Veröffentlichungen der Arbeitsgemeinschaft für das Archiv- und Bibliothekswesen in der Evangelischen Kirche*, Bd. 8. Neustadt an der Aisch: Degener, 1971. A 336 page bibliography of essays on Protestant topics found in festschriften on German churchmen and scholars.

**2-041** *Estudios Biblicos*. 2nd series, Vol. 1- . Madrid: Librería Científica Medinaceli for the Instituto Francisco Suárez of the Consejo Superior de Investigaciones Científicas, 1941- . A quarterly publication with a Spanish Catholic bias in its selection of book reviews and essays from 80 journals. Contains annual index of authors.

**2-042** Fitzmyer, Joseph A. *The Dead Sea Scrolls: Major Publications and Tools for Study*. SBLSBS 8. Scholars Press, 1975. A well-indexed guide for the beginner to materials on the Dead Sea Scrolls.

**2-043** Glanzman, George S. and Joseph A. Fitzmyer. *An Introductory Bibliography for the Study of Scripture*. Woodstock Papers, Occasional Essays for Theology 5. Westminster, MD: Newman Press, 1961. Intended for use mainly by Roman Catholic seminarians, the citations and annotations in this 21-section volume have been selected from periodicals, series, texts and Bible versions, lexicons, grammars, concordances, commentaries in series, dictionaries, subject aspects, NT Apocrypha, rabbinical literature on the NT and bibliography. A helpful volume that presents materials important in the study of scripture. Contains author index and list of abbreviations. The work was revised after Glanzman's death and a second edition appeared in 1981 (published by the Editrice Pontificio Instituto Biblico); a third edition appeared as *Subsidia biblica* 3 in 1990.

2-044       Gottcent, John H. *The Bible as Literature: A Selective Bibliography.* Boston: G. K. Hall and Company, 1979. A well-annotated guide for beginners to books, articles, and dissertations on the Bible as literature published/reissued between 1950-1978. Contains cross-references, author index, subject index.

2-045       Herbert, Arthur Sumner. *Historical Catalogue of Printed Editions of the English Bible, 1525-1961: Revised and Expanded from the Edition of T. H. Darlow and H. F. Moule, 1903.* New York: American Bible Society; London: British and Foreign Bible Society, 1968. This expanded volume has entries from ten additional British and American libraries noted for their Bible collections. Chronologically arranged by date of publication.

2-046       Hester, Goldia (comp. and ed.). *Guide to Bibles in Print.* Austin, TX: Richard Gordon and Associates, 1966- . An annual publication, this current guide to Bibles in print contains complete descriptions from publisher's catalogues.

2-047       Hester, James and Genevieve Kelly (eds.). *The Tools of Biblical Interpretation: A Bibliographical Guide.* Corvina, CA: American Baptist Seminary of the West, 1968. Reflecting conservative Protestant views of biblical studies, this volume contains bibliographical essays and lists by Baptist academics and theological students.

2-048       Hester, James and Genevieve Kelly (eds.). *The Tools of Biblical Interpretation: A Bibliographical Guide. Supplement, 1968-1970.* Corvina, CA: American Baptist Seminary of the West, 1970. Supplement to entry **2-047**. An important additional resource book.

## New Testament Bibliographies

2-049       Aune, David E. *Jesus and the Synoptic Gospels: An Introductory Bibliographical Study Guide and Syllabus.* Madison, WI: Theological Students Fellowship, 1980. The first of a new series of study guides, this guide to literature on the various ways of studying the relations of Jesus to the Synoptic Gospels is well annotated.

2-050          Bowman, John Wick (ed.). *Bibliography of New Testament Literature*. San Anselmo, CA: San Francisco Theological Seminary, 1954. A mimeographed listing of 2,400 books and articles. The entries are annotated and are arranged by topic. Includes an author index and covers 1920-1950.

2-051          De Marco, Angelus A. *The Tomb of St. Peter: A Representative and Annotated Bibliography of the Excavations*. NovTSup 8. Leiden: Brill, 1968. An important guide to specific areas of NT history, this interesting bibliography contains 870 entries from monographs and periodicals. Contains author index.

2-052          Doty, William G. *The Discipline and Literature of Form Criticism: A Bibliographical Lecture*. Evanston, IL: Garrett Theological Seminary Library, 1967. This classified list of 215 articles provides an excellent overview of the early development in form criticism.

2-053          Duplacy, J. A continuing bibliography of NT textual criticism has been published in *Biblica* (**3-010**) since 1968 (vol. 49). These bi-annual bibliographies are published in 2 parts so that one part appears in each two year cycle. Duplacy's earlier bibliographies were published in *Recherches de Science Religieuse*, 1962-1966.

2-054          France, R. T. (ed.). *A Bibliographical Guide to New Testament Research*. Cambridge: Tyndale House, 1974. Third edition published in 1979 by JSOT Press. First issued in duplicated form (1968) and later reprinted in *Themelios* V (1969), 11-31, it was first published by Tyndale in 1974. General in nature, it makes no attempt to reference works in the more central areas of NT criticism, exegesis, or theology. It covers mainly British authors though some attention is given to American and continental writers.

2-055          Gaffron, H.-G. and H. Stegemann. *Systematisches Verzeichnis der wichtigsten Fachliteratur für das Theologiestudium: Vorausdruck für das Einzelfach Neues Testament germäss dem Stand im Frühjahr 1966*. Bonn: H. Bouvier & Co., 1966. A handy reference tool for any level student, this volume is a brief annotated list of essential works to be consulted in the study of the NT. Contains author index.

2-056          Hadidian, D. Y. *A Periodical and Monographic Index to the Literature of the Gospels and Acts based on the files of the*

*École Biblique in Jerusalem.* Bibliographia
Tripotomopolitana 3. Pittsburgh: The Clifford E. Barbour
Library, Pittsburgh Theological Seminary, 1971. A limited
guide covering 80 years of biblical scholarship through
1968, the list covers 80 periodicals and contains 2,300
articles on the Gospels and Acts.

2-057        Humphreys, H. M. *A Bibliography for the Gospel of Mark: 1954-
             1980.* Studies in the Bible and Early Christianity 1. New
             York/Toronto: The Edwin Mellen Press, 1981. This
             exhaustive work contains a helpful classification of
             materials as well as a brief annotation.

2-058        Kissinger, Warren S. *The Parables of Jesus: A History of
             Interpretation and Bibliography.* American Theological
             Library Association Bibliography Series 4. Metuchen, NJ:
             Scarecrow Press, 1979. Valuable for the beginner and for
             advanced study, this guide begins with a series of surveys
             on the history of parable interpretation from Irenaeus to the
             present and contains a substantial bibliography of relevant
             books and articles in European languages. Contains subject
             and author indices.

2-059        Kissinger, Warren S. *The Sermon on the Mount: A History of
             Interpretation and Bibliography.* American Theological
             Library Association Bibliography Series 3. Metuchen, NJ:
             Scarecrow Press, 1975. A useful tool for undergraduates
             (extensive essay on the history of interpretation of the
             Sermon from the patristic period to the present) and
             advanced students (bibliography containing 2,500 entries
             covering texts, criticism, interpretation and sermons), this
             volume contains a general index and an index of biblical
             references. An appendix lists the sermon in 61 languages.

2-060        Langevin, P.-E.  (ed.).  *Bibliographie biblique. Biblical
             Bibliography. Biblische Bibliographie. Bibliografía biblica.
             Bibliografía biblica I: 1930-1970; II: 1930-1975; III: 1930-
             1983.* Quebec: L'Université Laval, 1972[1]; 1978[2]; 1985[3].
             These are three large tomes with hefty price tags of well
             over $100 each, but they do contain a wealth of information
             arranged in a very convenient format. Volume I consists of
             the systematic indexing of the contents of 70 Catholic
             periodicals published between 1930-1970. The languages
             covered are English, French, German, Spanish, Portuguese,
             and Italian. Also, there are references to the articles

contained in 286 multi-authored works that appeared in this same period. This massive task translates into over 21,000 entries though frequently the same entry appears in more than a single classification. Volume II brings these forward five years, but adds about 50 other important, non-Catholic journals for the years 1930-1975, and the contents of 812 works published in the same period. This volume contains another 23,000 plus citations. Volume III adds another 43 journals and updates all previous journals through 1983; also adds the contents of another 450 multi-authored works.

2-061 Lyons, William Nelson (ed.). *New Testament Literature in 1940.* Chicago, IL: New Testament Club of the University of Chicago, 1941. The work is comprised of brief abstracts or annotations, most of which are highly critical, and is arranged by subject. Contains no index.

2-062 Lyons, William Nelson (ed.). *New Testament Literature, 1941.* Chicago IL: New Testament Club of the University of Chicago, 1942. Continuation of entry **2-061** mentioned above increasing to 97 the number of periodicals indexed.

2-063 Lyons, William Nelson and Merril M. Parvis (eds.). *New Testament Literature: An Annotated Bibliography, 1943-1945.* Chicago, IL: University of Chicago Press, 1974. Indexed by authors, Greek words, and biblical texts, this comprehensive bibliography contains 3,432 entries which are international in scope.

2-064 Malatesta, Edward. *St. John's Gospel 1920-1965: A Cumulative and Classified Bibliography of Book and Periodical Literature on the Fourth Gospel.* AnBib 32. Rome: Pontifical Biblical Institute, 1967. A compilation of materials dealing with the Gospel of St. John from 50 volumes of *Elenchus bibliographicus biblica* (**2-039**), this volume contains books, articles, and book reviews in a classified sequence. See also Van Belle, *Johannine Bibliography, 1966-1985* (**2-079**) which carries forward Malatesta's work.

2-065 Marrow, S. B. *Basic Tools of Biblical Exegesis: A Student's Manual.* Subsidia biblica 2. 2nd ed. Rome: Editrice Pontificio Instituto Biblico, 1978. Aims to assist students in their beginning work in exegesis. Lists 215 works it describes as the basic tools needed for the work of exegesis.

2-066       Mattill, A. J., Jr. and M. B. Mattill (eds.). *A Classified Biblio-graphy of Literature on the Acts of the Apostles.* NTTS 7. Leiden: Brill; Grand Rapids: Eerdmans, 1966. This volume contains 6,646 entries from 180 periodicals and includes titles of NT introductions and theologies, book reviews, homiletic and devotional works, and dictionary articles.

2-067       Metzger, B. M. *Annotated Bibliography of Textual Criticism of the New Testament, 1914-1939.* Studies and Documents 18. Copenhagen: Ejnar Munksgaard Verlag, 1955. Covering the period 1914-1939, this volume contains entries from 1,188 books monographs, articles, and dissertations. Contains index of names.

2-068       Metzger, B. M. *Index of Articles on the New Testament and the Early Church Published in Festschriften.* SBLMS 5. Philadelphia: Society of Biblical Literature, 1951. Thi is an important tool for uncovering important—but sometimes overlooked—articles in festschriften.

2-069       Metzger, B. M. *Index of Articles on the New Testament and the Early Church Published in Festschriften: Supplementary Volume.* Philadelphia: Society of Biblical Literature, 1955. Supplement to **2-068** above which updates and corrects the original volume.

2-070       Metzger, B. M. (ed.). *Index to Periodical Literature on the Apostle Paul.* NTTS 1. Leiden: Brill; Grand Rapids: Eerdmans, 1960. An indispensable tool for the study of the Pauline corpus, this bibliography contains 2,987 entries from 114 periodicals grouped conveniently under useful subject headings such as bibliographical articles on Paul, historical studies on the life of Paul, critical studies on Pauline literature, Pauline apocrypha, theological studies, history of the interpretation of Paul, and his letters.

2-071       Metzger, B. M. (ed.). *Index to Periodical Literature on Christ and the Gospels.* NTTS 6. Leiden: Brill, 1966. An indispensable tool for the study of the Gospels, this volume contains 10,090 entries from 160 periodicals under headings such as bibliographical articles on Christ and the Gospels; historical studies of the life of Jesus; critical studies of the Gospels, early non-canonical literature related to Christ and the Gospels; theological studies concerning Jesus Christ and the

Gospels; influence and interpretation of Jesus Christ and the
Gospels in worship, fine arts, and culture in general.

2-072        Mills, Watson E. *Bibliographies for Biblical Research*. Vol. 1. *The
Gospel according to Matthew*; Vol. 2. *The Gospel
according to Mark*; Vol. 3. *The Gospel according to Luke*;
Vol. 4. *The Gospel according to John*. Lewiston, NY:
Mellen Biblical Press, 1993-1994. These volumes range in
size from about 2,500 to 4,000 entries. The entries are
arranged in sections: by verse citation, by subject, and
commentaries.

2-073        Mills, Watson E. *A Bibliography of the Periodical Literature on
the Acts of the Apostles 1962-1984*. NovTSup 58. Leiden:
Brill, 1986. This index carries forward the Mattills' work
though only periodicals are included.

2-074        Mills, Watson E. *Index to Periodical Literature on the Apostle
Paul*. Leiden: Brill, 1993. This index carries forward the
work of Metzger **(2-071)** through 1992.

2-075        *New Testament Abstracts*. Vol. 1- . Weston College, MA. An
abstracting service covering nearly 400 Catholic, Protestant,
and Jewish periodicals, this journal is an indispensable
reference tool for biblical scholars. Cumulative indices. The
most comprehensive and thus indispensable volume in
English for those wanting to keep abreast of the flood of
new literature appearing in numerous journals in several
languages.

2-076        Neirynck, F., et al. *The Gospel of Mark: A Cumulative Bibliography 1950-1990*. BETL 102. Louvain: Peeters, 1988. This
volume is arranged alphabetically by author with extensive
scriptural and subject indices. The listings are virtually
definitive for anything published after 1950.

2-077        Parvis, Merril M. (ed.). *New Testament Literature in 1942*.
Chicago, IL: New Testament Club of the University of
Chicago, 1943. Arranged by subject, most of the 500 entries
are fully annotated. Contains author index; excludes
European works.

2-078        Scholer, David M. *A Basic Bibliographic Guide for New Testament
Exegesis*. 2nd ed. Grand Rapids: Eerdmans, 1971. Primarily
for theological students, this useful volume is restricted to
English titles. Entries are briefly annotated.

2-079    Van Belle, G. *Johannine Bibliography, 1966-1985*. BETL 82.
         Louvain: Peeters, 1988. Carries forward the earlier work of
         E. Malatesta (**2-064**).

2-080    Van Segbroeck, F. *The Gospel of Luke: A Cumulative Bibliography
         1973-1988*. BETL 88. Louvain: Peeters, 1989.

2-081    Wagner, G. (ed.). *New Testament Exegetical Bibliographical Aids*.
         Rüschlikon, Switzerland: Baptist Theological Seminary,
         1973- . Bibliography of interpretations of NT passages from
         biblical journals and monographs. On index cards, these
         entries exist in a first and second series. Three volumes
         have been published: Matthew-Mark; Luke-Acts; Johannine
         Writings. Available from Mercer University Press, Macon,
         Georgia. The published volumes represent a collation of the
         first series and the second series.

# CHAPTER 3

# Periodicals

One important resource for students doing biblical research is the scholarly journal. Periodicals represent the leading edge of the new work being done in a specific area. Often times these articles describe a new thesis that is in the initial stage of development. The idea is shared via the journal with other colleagues who are frequently ready to critique the new work. Journals are thus a proving ground for ideas, concepts, and methodologies that must be further refined and enlarged before being offered to the scholarly world as a book or monograph.

3-001      *Andrews University Seminary Studies* (AUSS). This English language journal is published quarterly by professors of the Seventh-Day Adventist Seminary at Andrews University. Includes articles on both the OT and NT and related fields such as archaeological reviews. Also includes book reviews of current literature.

3-002    *Australian Biblical Review* (ABR). This English language journal is published by the Fellowship for Biblical Studies, Melbourne University, Department of Semitic Studies. Includes articles and reviews.

3-003    *Bibbia e Oriente* (BibO). Published in Italian six times a year, this journal includes articles on both the OT and NT. Also includes brief philological notes although these are often very technical.

3-004    *Bibel et vie chrétienne* (BVC). This French language journal is published four to six times a year by the Belgian Benedictines of the Abbey of Maredsous. It features articles on the OT and NT as well as reviews. The journal is popular in scope and focuses mainly upon the practical side of biblical studies, such as preaching, spirituality, and liturgy.

3-005    *Bibel und Kirch* (BK). This journal probes the impact of the Bible upon church life. Published four times a year in German.

3-006    *Bibel und Leben* (BibL). This quarterly, German language journal intends to stimulate discussion and understanding of modern biblical interpretation. Edited by top-ranking German Catholic OT and NT Scholars.

3-007    *Bible et Terre sainte* (BTS). The French language counterpart of the *Biblical Archaeologist* (BA; **3-011**). This journal appears nine times a year and contains popular articles accompanied by excellent photographs on topics pertaining to the history and archaeology of both the OT and the NT.

3-008    *The Bible Translator* (BT). This journal offers articles on the difficulties that confront the Bible translator. Published by the United Bible Society, it contains very technical articles dealing with the meaning of words, phrases, and the details of syntax as these bear upon biblical translation.

3-009    *Bible und Liturgie* (BL). Published six times a year in German, this periodical is dedicated to the study of the relationship between Scripture and Roman Catholic liturgy. Primarily for clergy and laity.

3-010    *Biblica* (B). Published quarterly by the Pontifical Biblical Institute. Articles on both the OT and NT; shorter notes; reviews. One of the most important journals in biblical studies. It carries articles in Italian, Latin, and Spanish. Until it became a free-standing volume in own right in 1967, the *Elenchus bibliographicus biblicus* (**2-039**) was a part of *Biblica*.

3-011    *The Biblical Archaeologist* (BA). An English language journals is published quarterly by the American Schools of Oriental Research and contains articles relating to both the OT and the NT. There are some occasional reviews. The journal aims to keep the reader abreast of current features, reports, and articles on archaeological discovery, work, and interpretation, as these bear on the study of the Bible.

3-012    *Biblical Interpretation: A Journal of Contemporary Approaches* (BI). This is a new journal. It's first issue appeared in 1993. It features articles on new types of biblical exegesis such as narrative criticism, feminist criticism and liberation hermeneutics. Published by Brill.

3-013    *Biblical Research* (BRes). Written and published annually by the Chicago Society of Biblical Research. Contains articles on both the OT and the NT.

3-014    *Biblical Theology Bulletin* (BTB). This periodical was begun after the discontinuation of *Verbum domini* (VD; **3-037**), and appeared both in English and French. First published only three times a year, it has become a quarterly only in English and is mainly for those who want "instant" biblical theology.

3-015    *Biblische Zeitschrift* (BZ). Publishes articles in German, French, and English twice yearly, this periodical is the leading Roman Catholic biblical journal in the German-speaking world. Contains articles on both the OT and the NT, biblical news, and reviews. It was begun in 1903 and its first series ceased publication in 1939. A new series was begun in 1957 and continues today.

3-016    *The Catholic Biblical Quarterly* (CBQ). Published by the Catholic Biblical Association, this journal contains articles on both the OT and the NT, shorter notes, biblical news; archaeological reports, reviews and short notices on books in the biblical field.

3-017        *Coniectanea neotestamentica* (ConN). Sporadically published in
             Swedish, German, French, and English, some issues are
             monographs and some present a collection of articles by
             various NT scholars.

3-018        *Cultura Bíblica* (CultB). Published in Spanish, this popular
             quarterly publication is the counterpart of *EstBib* (**3-021**).
             Contains articles on both the OT and the NT, biblical news,
             and reviews.

3-019        *Elenchus of Biblica* (1985- ), formerly *Elenchus bibliographicus
             biblicus* (**2-039**). Once a part of *Biblica* (**3-010**), since 1968
             it has been published separately. Greatly expanded and
             improved; an indispensable tool. R. North has been the
             compiler of *EB* since P. Nobler's death in 1980. This
             massive work usually appears two or three years after its
             title date. It includes no abstracts or annotation; however,
             the cataloguing of the entries is meticulous and precise
             according to divisions that seem confusing at first, but
             which can be learned with little difficulty. The *EB* contains
             references to periodical and monograph publications as well
             as multi-authored works, dissertations, and book reviews.

3-020        *Ephemerides Theologicae Lovanienses* (ETL). Published quarterly,
             this scholarly journal is a general survey of theological
             studies and contains material from books and articles from
             approximately 500 journals. Also contains author index,
             detailed summary of the subject headings used, full listing
             of periodicals (including addresses), and each entry provides
             basic but sufficient bibliographical information.

3-021        *Estudios biblicos* (EstBib). Published quarterly in Spanish, this
             journal contains articles on both the OT and the NT, shorter
             notes, and reviews. Good biblical journal for Spanish
             readers.

3-022        *Internationale Zeitschriftenchau für Bibelwissenschaft und
             Grezgebiete* (IZBG). Published annually since 1952, this
             journal lists biblical articles and provides abstracts in
             German. Contains author index.

3-023        *Interpretation: A Journal of Bible and Theology* (Interp). Published
             quarterly in English as a continuation of *Union Seminary
             Review* (USR), this journal contains articles on both the OT
             and the NT, reviews, and shorter notes.

**3-024**    *Journal of Biblical Literature* (JBL). Greatly improved in quality over the years, this journal is published quarterly in English (with an occasional French or German contribution). Contains articles on both the OT and the NT, shorter notes, reviews, summaries of books of collected essays.

**3-025**    *Journal of Religious and Theological Information* (JRTI). A new journal begun in 1993. It publishes articles that pertain to the production, dissemination, preservation, and bibliography of theological and religious information.

**3-026**    *Journal for the Study of the New Testament* (JSNT). Published in English, this journal contains articles and reviews on the NT. *JSNT* also publishes a supplement series of monographs.

**3-027**    *New Testament Studies* (NTSt). Published quarterly in English, French, and German, the contributors to this journal are among the best in the field of the NT representing all faiths. Contains articles on the NT and related fields, short studies, and a list of the names and addresses of membership of Society of New Testament Studies.

**3-028**    *Novum Testamentum* (NovT). Published quarterly. The articles and reviews are in English, French, and German. *NovT* publishes a monograph series (*NovTSup*).

**3-029**    *Qadmoniot* (Qad). This beautifully illustrated journal is published quarterly in modern Hebrew for the antiquities of Israel and biblical lands. Surveys the archaeological work done each year at various sites. Contains up-to-date information on Jerusalem.

**3-030**    *Revista biblica* (RevB). Published quarterly in Spanish, it contains articles on both the OT and the NT, reviews, bulletins, biblical news and church documents on Scripture. More popular than technical.

**3-031**    *Rivista biblica* (RivB). Published in Italian, this quarterly publication on both the OT and the NT contains short notes, bulletins, and reviews. Published by the Italian Biblical Association.

**3-032**    *Revue biblique* (RB). Published quarterly. Most articles are in French, occasionally in English. The journal contains articles on both the OT and the NT, chronicles of archaeological work on biblical lands; shorter and longer reviews of significant books on both the OT and the NT.

3-033    *Revue de Qumran* (RevQ). Devoted to the study of the Dead Sea Scrolls, this journal has attempted, somewhat unsuccessfully, to encourage scholars to publish in one centralized organ. Each issue contains a valuable, but complicated, bibliography. Also contains index.

3-034    *Scripture Bulletin* (ScrB). A quarterly publication on both the OT and NT, this popular journal contains Biblical news, articles of practical interest about the Bible, information about new archaeological discoveries in the Holy Land, news of pilgrimages to the Bible Lands, book reviews, and answers to questions on Biblical matters posed by its readership.

3-035    *Semeia: An Experimental Journal for Biblical Criticism* (Semeia). Published at irregular intervals, this journal contains articles on both the OT and the NT.

3-036    *Svensk exegetisk årsbok* (SEÅ). Published in Swedish, this annual is devoted to the exegetical studies of passages in both the OT and the NT.

3-037    *Verbum domini* (VD). Published until 1969. Contained articles on both the OT and the NT, reviews, and was an extensive survey of biblical periodicals and collected works.

3-038    *Vetus Testamentum* (VT). Published quarterly in English, French, and German, mainly contains articles on the OT with an occasional article on Judaism; also contains short notes and reviews.

3-039    *Zeitschrift für die neutestamentliche Wissenschaft und die Kunde des Urchristentums* (ZNW). Published twice a year in German and (occasionally) English, this publication contains articles and short notes on the NT and related fields.

# CHAPTER 4

# Indexing and Abstracting

Indexing and abstracting services have arisen in the face of the proliferation of the various journals in the field on NT studies. Even if an individual scholar could afford to subscribe to all of them and if the language facility were present, no one would have enough time to read the voluminous materials contained in the pages of these publications.

The indexing and abstracting services provide help by using a large staff of indexers and abstracters to identify and catalogue these materials so that the researcher need only read those publications that meet his/her research interests.

There are two types of indexing services available: (1) regularly published services such as *New Testament Abstracts* (**4-007**), and (2) computer searches.[1]

The regularly published indices arrange listed materials by various schema such as by scriptural citations, subject area, and books of the Bible. For instance, if a researcher was examining the "Sermon on the Mount," he/she might look in the scriptural index for Matthew 5, 6, 7, and in the subject area for the following:

Lord's Prayer

Beatitudes

Sermon on the Mount

Teachings of Jesus

Parables

Some searches may be conducted by computer so that the researcher, after supplying search/match quantifiers, receives a printout of all of the articles/books contained in a specific database on that specific subject AS DEFINED by the qualifiers. These qualifiers, or "key words" as they are sometimes called, will enable the computer to select (or reject) certain information for the final printout that has been tailored to the specific research interest.

For instance, suppose you were preparing a dissertation proposal on the "we" sections in Acts and wanted to generate as complete a list as possible of work done in this area since 1960. You would define your search to include the years 1960-present, and to include articles, monographs, books, and edited

---

[1]For further discussion of on-line computer based-searches, see Regazzi, John J. and Theodore C. Hines, *A Guide to Indexed Periodicals in Religion* (Metuchen, NJ: The Scarecrow Press, Inc., 1975) (**4-009**).

collections of essays including festschriften. You would then enter the following quantifiers:

"we" sections

Luke, author of Acts

Sources of Acts

Acts, sources of

Luke's relationship to Paul

The materials reviewed in this chapter include the major "hard copy" indexing and abstracting journals, as well as the major on-line computer services.

4-001     Berlin, Charles. *Index to Festschriften in Jewish Studies.* New York: KATV, 1971. Volume lists 6,700 articles from 243 festschriften. Complete with bibliography, author index, subject index. Article information gives author, title, name of honoree, and pagination.

4-002     *Bibliographie Biblique.* Montréal: Les Facultés de Théologie et de Philosophie de la compagnie de Jesus, 1958. A subject index to Roman Catholic periodicals and books in French, English, and Latin. Consists of more than 9,000 entries from 29 Catholic periodicals published between 1920-1957.

4-003     *The Catholic Periodical and Literature Index (CPLI).* A bimonthly publication, this is a continuation of *The Catholic Periodical Index*, a cumulative author and subject index to selected Roman Catholic periodicals.

4-004     *Christian Periodical Index: An Index to Subjects, Authors, and Book Reviews.* Published quarterly with triennial cumulations. Limited to titles produced in North America and Britain, this is a subject index to approximately 40 periodicals and journals of interest to evangelical and conservative Protestants.

4-005       *Guide to Social Science and Religion in Periodical Literature.*
            Entries are listed by subject only without benefit of
            cross-reference or author index. Poorly duplicates work of
            other indices.

4-006       *Mosher Periodical Index.* A monthly publication containing articles
            from 250 periodicals, the index is created as soon as each
            journal is received in Mosher Library. Contains author
            index.

4-007       *New Testament Abstracts.* This publication provides abstracts on all
            articles on the NT from 250 periodicals.

4-008       *A Periodical and Monographic Index to the Literature on the
            Gospels and Acts Based on the Files of the Ecole Biblique
            in Jerusalem.* Listed by specific passages of scripture, this
            index contains articles and monographs on the Gospels and
            Acts from 80 scholarly periodicals.

4-009       Regazzi, John J. and Theodore C. Hines. *A Guide to Indexed
            Periodicals in Religion.* Metuchen, NJ: Scarecrow Press,
            1975. This publication is a valuable tool for tracing
            information through seventeen major indexing and
            abstracting services. It lists, alphabetically, 2,700 periodicals
            indicating which indexing and abstracting services cover
            each title.

4-010       *Religion Index One: Periodicals: A Subject Index to Periodical
            Literature, Including an Author Index with Abstracts, and
            a Book Review Index.* Semiannual with biennial
            cumulations. With a slight Protestant bias and a clear
            preference for North American journals, this is an
            alphabetical subject index to articles from more than 200
            periodicals. Contains some abstracts, an author index, and
            book review index (arranged alphabetically by author). This
            service is available on CD-ROM with annual updates.

4-011       *Religion Index Two: Multi-Author works.* Annual. A complement
            to *Religion Index One* (**4-010**), this volume treats articles in
            conference     proceedings,     festschriften,     and     similar
            collections. Contains bibliographical list of titles indexed,
            alphabetical subject guide to articles, author and editor
            index.

4-012       *Religious Books and Serials in Print.* Published on an irregular
            basis, this is a comprehensive listing of currently available

American publications on all religions, metaphysics, theology, ethics, and related subjects of both philosophical and practical orientation. Contains indices of subjects, authors, titles, and series.

4-013   *Religious Periodicals Index.* Quarterly. Index of major American religious journals covering titles not found in the *Catholic Periodical Index* or ATLA index.

4-014   *Religious and Theological Abstracts.* Quarterly. A guide to theological literature, this service treats articles from more than 160 major religious periodicals in a classified sequence of five main fields: biblical, theological, historical, practical, and sociological. Fourth issue contains subject, author, and scripture indices. Available on CD-ROM with annual updates.

4-015   Rounds, Dorothy. *Articles on Antiquity in Festschriften.* Cambridge: Harvard University Press, 1962. Complexly arranged (explanation provided), this volume contains 1,178 entries on the ancient near east, OT, Greece, Rome, Roman Law, NT, and early church, Byzantium, and Western Europe in the Middle Ages. (The author recognizes the work of Bruce Metzger and does not repeat his entries [2-067]).

4-016   *St. John's University Library Index to Biblical Journals.* Collegeville, MN: St. John's University Press, 1971. Covering the last 50 years, this is a computer-generated cumulative index to some of the major journals.

4-017   Sayre, John L. and Roberta Hamburger. *An Index of Festschriften in Religion.* Enid, OK: Seminary Press, 1970. Indices by author and title the articles in 84 festschriften, many of which are not found in Metzger (2-068, 2-069). There are more than 1,500 entries. Also, see an update published in 1973 that lists and additional 71 festschriften. Each volume is arranged under Library of Congress subject headings (refer to Chapter 16).

# CHAPTER 5

# Book Reviews

Book reviews afford timely insight into emerging methodologies and interpretations. Since there is often an interval of several months to a few years between the publication of a title and its review, it is imperative that reviews be noted as soon as they appear. To assist in locating reviews several services are available, e.g., *New Testament Abstracts* (**4-007**) and *Elenchus of Biblica* (**3-019**).

**5-001**     *Book Review Digest: An Index to Reviews of Current Books.* Vol. 1- . New York: H. W. Wilson Company, 1905- ; monthly with quarterly and annual cumulations. Covering nearly 100 American and British periodicals, entries are arranged alphabetically by author with publication details. Entries contain a brief description and excerpts from selected reviews. Subject and title indices available.

5-002          *Book Review Index.* Vol. 1- . Detroit: Gale Research Co., 1965- .
               Listed alphabetically by author, the journals contains more
               than 30,000 entries from 300 American publications. The
               entries cover a wide range of subjects including humanities,
               social sciences, fiction, poetry, etc.

5-003          *Book Reviews of the Month.* Vol. 1- . Ft. Worth: Southwestern
               Baptist Theological Seminary, Fleming Library, 1962- .
               Arranged first by subject under the Dewey Decimal
               Classification system (refer to Chapter 16), then
               alphabetically by author, the staff of the library has
               compiled a ready reference to reviews of books in about
               eighty selected periodicals, mostly related to theological
               studies. Author index annually.

5-004          Mills, Watson E. (ed.). *Index to Review of New Testament Books
               Between 1900-1950.* Danville, VA: Association of Baptist
               Professors of Religion, 1977. Together with *New Testament
               Abstracts* (**4-007**), this book attempts to catalogue critical
               reviews from the beginning of the 20th century within a
               specialized area of biblical studies. A tool for the student in
               evaluating a particular book by providing a sample of
               reaction to it at the time of its publication.

5-005          *Religious Book Review.* Vol. 1- . Roslyn Heights, NY: Religious
               Book Review Press, 1958- ; semiannual. Reflecting a strong
               Roman Catholic interest, it is especially useful as a guide
               to North American publications of interest to Catholics.
               Contains articles on the religious book trade, libraries, and
               authors of interest in religious circles, information and notes
               on new books.

5-006          *Religious Book Review Index.* Vol. 1- . Calcutta: K. K. Roy
               (private), Ltd., 1970- ; bimonthly. A checklist of reviews of
               current religious books covered in three of the
               approximately 400 theological reviews scanned for the
               index within 18 months of the book's publication.

5-007          *Religious Studies Review: A Quarterly Review of Publications in
               the Field of Religion and Related Disciplines.* Vol. 1- .
               Valparaiso, IN: Council of Societies for the Study of
               Religion, 1975- ; quarterly. Reviewing some 1,200 titles
               annually, each issue contains review essays and shorter
               booknotes arranged under specific subject headings. For
               example, one issue contains "Dissertations in Progress,"

another includes "Dissertations Completed," with an annual index in issue for each year.

# CHAPTER 6

# Dissertations and Theses

The term "dissertation" is used generally to refer to the finished research project completed in fulfillment of the requirements for a doctoral degree, whereas the term "thesis" applies to the research done for a master's degree.

Graduate dissertations and theses offer a wealth of information and bibliography to the researcher. For example, a researcher will find that dissertations provide an excellent source for a quick review of the current research in a given area. These writings often provide detailed bibliographies and sometimes suggest alternative, or new, methodologies for studying traditional problems. Dissertations often assist in identifying new scholars whose work may not otherwise be readily available.

The problems in utilizing these marvelous resources consist of locating relevant dissertations and theses and then obtaining copies of them. Many major theological libraries located at seminaries, colleges, and universities where graduate work is offered simply buy every new dissertation that is produced. Rather than dealing with each individual institution where graduate work is offered, libraries order these dissertations through University Microfilms, Inc. The problem is that not all degree-granting institutions submit all dissertations to UMI. In those cases, it is best to consult one of the abstracting services listed below.

Many of these "location" services have concentrated on doctoral level dissertations, i.e., *Dissertation Abstracts* (**6-008**). Master's level theses represent a long-neglected area where the researcher may find dependable and relevant materials. Location is the key problem. One new effort in this direction is the Theological Research Exchange Network (TREN). This service is offered through Microfilm Service Company of Portland (5420 N.E. Glisan, Portland, Oregon [503-239-0570]). TREN makes available all theses from member institutions on microfiche. Presently, the member institutions include: Dallas Theological Seminary; Western Conservative Baptist Seminary; Bob Jones University; Mulnomah School of the Bible; Western Evangelical Seminary; Trinity Evangelical Seminary; Calvin Theological Seminary; Reformed Theological Seminary; and Grace Theological Seminary.


**6-001**        *American Doctoral Dissertations.* University Microfilms
                 International, 1964/1965- . Replaces *Doctoral Dissertations
                 Accepted by American Universities* (1933/1934-1954/1955)
                 and *Index to American Doctoral Dissertations* (1954/1955-
                 1963/1964). The entries are arranged alphabetically by
                 subject and then by university under each topic. No
                 abstracts are included. There is an author index.

**6-002**        Bilboul, Roger R. (ed.). *Retrospective Index to Theses of Great
                 Britain and Ireland, 1716-1950.* 5 vols. American

Bibliographical Center/Clio Press, 1975-1977. This work is a supplement to the *Index to Theses Accepted for Higher Degrees by Universities of Great Britain and Ireland and the Council of National Academic Awards*. As such it lists theses accepted prior to 1950. The entries are arranged by subject. Volume 1 covers the humanities and includes an author index.

6-003     Black, Dorothy M. (comp.). *Guide to Lists of Master's Theses*. American Library Association, 1965. Lists theses by fields of study as well as by institution granting the degree.

6-004     Bonet-Maury, G. "Catalogue des thèses soutenues dans les facultés de theologie de langue francaise." *Encyclopédie des sciences religieuses*. Sandoz et Fischenbacher, 1877-1882. 13:235-300. Lists doctorate, license, and baccalaureate degrees. Arranged chronologically under the name of the university. Covers the period 1800 through 1882.

6-005     Buss, Martin John. *Old Testament Dissertations, 1928-1958*. University Microfilms, 1967. This volume covers the period before *Dissertation Abstracts International* (6-008) began appearing.

6-006     *Comprehensive Dissertation Index*. University Microfilms International, 1973- . This 37 volume cumulative listing of dissertations was written during the period 1861-1972. Volume 32 covers religion with approximately 417,000 titles listed. Entries are arranged by subject and then alphabetically by key word within each field. A 19 volume cumulative listing, with the same title, covers the period 1973-1977 (volume 16 of which has 178,000 entries in the area of religion).

6-007     Council on Graduate Studies in Religion. *Doctoral Dissertations in the Field of Religion: Their Titles, Location, Fields and Short Précis of Contents*. 2 vols. Columbia University Press, 1954-1961. The first volume covers the period 1940-1952 and the second covers 1952-1961. The listing is alphabetical by author with approximately 1,000 entries. There is a brief abstract for each entry. Presently, the author, title, and institution information collected by the CGSR is published in the *Religious Studies Review* (5-007), twice yearly as "Dissertations in Progress" and "Dissertations Completed." The listings are generally limited to CGSR member institutions although the *RelSR* includes a few listings from non-member institutions. There is a specific section, arranged by author, listing dissertations in the biblical studies area.

6-008        *Dissertations Abstracts International: Abstracts of Dissertations Available on Microfilm or as Xerographic Reproductions.* University Microfilms was originally called *Microfilm Abstracts* and later *Dissertation Abstracts*. Published in three parts, section A includes philosophy, religion, and theology. The publications reports on dissertations at more than 400 North American institutions. The listings consist of very complete abstracts (prepared by the author). For cumulative indices, see **6-006** and *Dissertation Abstracts International Retrospective Index.*

# CHAPTER 7

# Dictionaries

The idea of a dictionary of the Bible dates at least to Augustine who applauded "certain scholars" who had provided students of the scriptures "with interpretations of all Hebrew, Syrian, Egyptian, and other foreign expressions and names introduced without further explanation. . . . "[1] But Augustine knew that there would need to be additional categories of entries included before the task would be finished. He mentioned specifically "geographical locations, the flora and fauna, and the stones and unknown metals."[2]

---

[1]Doctrina Christiana, 2.39.

[2]Ibid.

But Augustine's dream was long in being realized. The first Bible dictionary of any importance did not appear until the early eighteenth century.[3] Written by a Benedictine monk, the work was translated into English in 1730 and published in a three-volume edition under the title *An Historical, Critical, Geographical, Chronological, and Etymological Dictionary of the Holy Bible.*

Since the eighteenth century there have been numerous Bible dictionaries produced, and they continue to appear in record numbers in the twentieth century. Typically, the more recent examples of these have been one-volume works[4] though one notable exception is the *Interpreter's Dictionary of the Bible* (7-004).[5] Because of a maximum length of about 1,000 2-column pages there are strict space limitations placed upon the various entries—a fact that the researcher must take into account when one of the dictionaries is consulted. Usually the more significant biblical terms are included, but general articles often replace individual articles, i.e., a general article on "musical instruments" would allude to the several specific instruments mentioned in scripture and thus there would not be individual entries for each.

7-001          *Biblisch-historisches Handwörterbuch.* Landeskunde, Geschichte, Religion, Kultur, Literatur, ed. B. Reicke & L. Ros. Vandenhoeck & Ruprecht, 1962-1966. 3 vols. Useful

---

[3] On the history and evolution of Bible dictionaries, see *The Jewish Encyclopedia* (New York: 1907) 4:577-79.

[4] The older dictionaries tend to be larger in terms of the number of volumes. The move toward the single volume dictionary may be a marketing consideration more than a conscious effort on the part of the editors. Many publishers hope these one volume dictionaries may replace or at least supplement the more traditional New Testament introductory volume in the college and seminary survey courses.

[5] In fact, the IDB is probably more accurately classified as an encyclopedia than a dictionary. As a rule, encyclopedias include biblical as well as theological materials.

background materials, and a little more wide-ranging on this than *The New Bible Dictionary* (**7-008**), but often thin.

**7-002**     Bromiley, G. W. (ed.). *International Standard Bible Encyclopedia.* 4 vols. Eerdmans, Vol. 1, 1979; Vol. 2, 1982; Vol 3, 1985; Vol. 4, in process. This completely revised version of *The International Standard Bible Encyclopedia* is as comprehensive and conservative as the original work. Broad coverage, selective (but current) bibliographies, and indexed maps make this a useful dictionary.

**7-003**     Bromiley, G. W. *Theological Dictionary of the New Testament Abridged in One Volume.* Eerdmans. This volume contains 15%-20% of the original. All Greek words have been transliterated: There are references throughout to the complete articles in *TDNT*.

**7-004**     Brown, Colin (ed.). *The New International Dictionary of New Testament Theology.* 3 vols. Exeter: Paternoster Press, 1975. Designed as a tool for critical Biblical study, this comprehensive dictionary of key NT theological terms is translated from the German *Theologisches Begriffslexicon zum Neuen Testament.* The addition of seventy major articles are arranged alphabetically under the English titles. An extensive glossary of technical terms is included at the front of volume 1; indices are provided at the end of volumes 1 and 2; a cumulative index is included in volume 3.

**7-005**     Buttrick, G. and K. Crim (eds.). *The Interpreter's Dictionary of the Bible.* 5 vols. Abingdon, 1986. The most widely-used Bible dictionary, the focus of this work is moderately technical. The list of contributors is impressive as are the bibliographies. Also contains maps and illustrations.

**7-006**     Cheyne, Thomas Kelly and J. Sutherland Black. *Encyclopaedia Biblica.* 4 vols. Macmillan, 1899-1903, 1977. The accuracy and scholarship of this monumental nineteenth-century work is beyond question. Containing a large number of contributors, signed articles and cross-references, the topics are arranged in alphabetical order with inserts of descriptive words or phrases. Written for either the scholar or the student.

**7-007**     Davis, J. D. (ed.). *Dictionary of the Bible.* Baker, [4]1954. Originally published in 1898, this work is badly outdated, even in the fourth edition. Despite this fact, because of its very traditional stance on many issues, it is widely reprinted in various editions.

7-008      Douglas, J. D. (ed.). *The New Bible Dictionary*. Tyndale, 1982. Popular with evangelicals and conservative readers, this is a major one-volume reference work that will please some readers and leave others looking for more refinement and discrimination on specific historical and geographic topics. Contains bibliographies.

7-009      *Eerdmans' Family Encyclopedia of the Bible*. Eerdmans, 1978. The best of dictionaries specifically designed for readers of all ages. The coverage is broad rather than deep, and the format is unusually attractive with ample illustrations. somewhat lightweight in terms of content. Also available in paperback.

7-010      Gehman, Henry Snyder (ed.). *The New Westminster Dictionary of the Bible*. Westminster Press, 1970. A scholarly one-volume work, conservative in its interpretation. Every proper name is phonetically transcribed and provided with diacritical marks in order that there may be no doubt about the correct pronunciation. Contains list of abbreviations, historical maps, and illustrations.

7-011      Hastings, James (ed.). *Dictionary of the Bible*. Rev. ed. by Frederick C. Grant and H. H. Rowley. Scribner, 1963. More comprehensive than *Harper's Bible Dictionary* (**7-015**), this work is arranged alphabetically, contains good outlines and headings, and is cross-referenced. Contains signed articles dealing with language, literature, and contents of the Bible along with Biblical theology.

7-012      Hillyer, N. (ed.). *The Illustrated Bible Encyclopedia*. 3 vols. InterVarsity, 1980. The test is that of the revised *The New Bible Dictionary* (**7-008**) with hundreds of illustrations in a pleasing and useful format: three columns to a page with a marginal column for the legends that identify the accompanying illustrations. This is a rare instance where adding illustrations, because it was done imaginatively, has improved the dictionary. For example, a color wheel is used to distinguish among the various colors described in the Bible, and the Greek and Hebrew terms used in each passage cited are given in transliteration. Although this is hardly a necessary piece of information, it is graphic and certainly engaging. The photographs are of stunning quality but not always relevant to the text under discussion. The line drawings are of medium detail, and these *are* relevant and appropriate. The bibliographies are selective, but they usually cite the basic literature. On the text itself, see the comments above.

7-013     Kittel, G. and George W. Bromiley (eds.). *Theological Dictionary of the New Testament.* 10 vols. Eerdmans, 1964-1976. This monumental work was begun by G. Kittel and later concluded by G. Friedrich. The original German edition was begun before WWII and the first four volumes appeared by 1942. Then came a twelve year hiatus before the appearance of volume 5 in 1954. In both the English and German editions, volume 10 is as an index volume; in the German, however, volume 10 updates to the secondary literature that is not found in the English edition. Many regard this work to be the single most important work for the study of the NT. The articles provide many exciting insights into the history and background of words, concepts, etc. including studies in etymology and usages in classical and Hellenistic Greek as well as LXX usage. Listing words, generally, alphabetical by roots, this work intends to provide the religious or theological significance of every major word in the Greek NT. Major attention is given to theological connotations. An extensive bibliography is provided at the bottom of every page. A "little" Kittel appeared in 1985.

7-014     McKenzie, J. L. *Dictionary of the Bible.* New York: Macmillan, 1965. McKenzie's work is far less well-known than it deserves to be. One has to admire it simply because it was *written*—not merely edited—by *one* person, and in only six years. The coverage is thorough and the writing is clear. Throughout, it serves the interests of the general reader. Here and there one notices a Roman Catholic position, but on the whole this is solid scholarship packaged appropriately for the non-specialist. It is not as up-to-date as *The New Bible Dictionary* (**7-008**), of course. With black-and-white photographs and adequate maps. Also available in paperback.

7-015     Miller, Madelein S. and J. Lane Miller. *Harper's Bible Dictionary.* New York: Harper, 1973. This work tries to define and describe all the major persons and places in the Bible. The dictionary is well-illustrated and includes a map section in the back. There is also an index to the illustrations.

7-016    Miller, Madelein S. and J. Lane Miller. *Harper's Encyclopedia of Bible Life.* New York: Harper, ³1955. This is an interesting book which tries to answer questions about biblical life such as: What does it look like? How did they dress? With what did they fight? What were their arts and crafts? This book includes a general index, maps, a map index, an index of biblical quotes, and an index of illustrations. The work is arranged in sections instead of the typical encyclopedic style.

7-017    Mills, Watson E. *Mercer Dictionary of the Bible.* Macon, GA: Mercer University Press, 1990. Now in its second printing, this volume was written by members of the National Association of Baptist Professors of Religion. It includes 64 pages of original color maps and plates. There are more than 1,300 articles and 200 black and white drawings, charts, and diagrams. Many articles include bibliography. There is an original outline for each book of the Bible and articles on the apocryphal books. Also published in the UK as *The Lutterworth Dictionary of the Bible* (Lutterworth Press, 1994).

7-018    Pfeiffer, C. F., H. F. Vos, and J. Rea (eds.). *Wycliffe Bible Encyclopedia.* 2 vols. Chicago: Moody Press, 1975. With more than 200 contributors, this set is for the non-specialist and offers good basic coverage of standard areas.

7-019    *Die Religion in Geschichte und Gegenwart.* Mohr, 3rd ed., 1957-1965. 7 vols. A mine of information, including many articles on NT subjects. Contains excellent bibliographies of German works. Usually abbreviated RGG.

7-020    Richardson, Alan. *A Theological Word Book of the Bible.* London: S.C.M. Press, 1950. Each of the 31 contributors, all specialists in their field, were asked to focus attention upon the theological meanings of the words and to use historical, geographical, archaeological, and philosophical details only as much as necessary for theological understanding. Words are listed alphabetically, and a simple cross-reference system is used. The work contains some bibliographies; all entries are signed.

7-021      Smith, W. and R. G. Lemmons, et al. (eds.). *New Smith's Bible Dictionary*. Garden City: Doubleday, 1966. Although there are several "Smith's" dictionaries, this is the original. It is very old, but comprehensive and noncontroversial, often containing more than one entry on a single topic to account for differing views.

7-022      Soulen, R. *Handbook of Biblical Criticism*. 2nd ed. Louisville, KY: John Knox Press, 1981. Many of the technical terms associated with the study of the Bible are examined here in detail. Very helpful for the novice.

7-023      Steinmueller, John E. (comp.). *Catholic Biblical Encyclopedia*. 2 vols. in 1. New York: Joseph F. Wagner, 1956. Covering a wide range of topics, this is the first Roman Catholic encyclopedia to be written in English. Combining two previous works, it is an accumulation of over 4,600 titles listed alphabetically in the OT section and 1,700 titles listed alphabetically in the NT section. Contains cross-references, maps, appendix. Limited in scope to the traditional orthodox faith of the Roman Catholic Church.

7-024      *Supplément au Dictionnaire de la Bible*. Originally ed. L. Pirot, now ed. H. Cazelles and A. Feuillet. Letouzey & Ané, 1928 ff. 9 vols. to date. Earlier fascicles of vol. 10 have reached into R. Earlier volumes now out of date, but more recent volumes provide excellent French Catholic scholarship, with full coverage of recent literature on each subject.

7-025      Tenney, M. C. (ed.). *The Zondervan Pictorial Bible Dictionary*. Grand Rapids: Zondervan. Rev. ed. 1963/1967. Lively entries get to the point in this dictionary, which was designed for pastors and church-school teachers. Its most obvious feature is hundreds of photographs; but the format is crowded and not very pleasing to the eye, and the entries are rather thin. The text of the Bible is the King James Version (with spellings from ASV and Revised Standard Version in parentheses). Ten printings in six years attest to the popularity of this dictionary. Also available with thumb index tabs.

7-026      Tenney, M. C. (ed.). *The Zondervan Pictorial Encyclopedia of the Bible*. 5 vols. Grand Rapids: Zondervan, 1975. The same basic editorial team that produced the *Zondervan Pictorial Bible Dictionary* (**7-025**) produced this more comprehensive work a decade later. It is a far more detailed guide, still lively in tone and much more pleasing visually, containing 32 pages of full-color maps, hundreds of diagrams, pictures, and black and white maps. Five volumes do not make the handiest format, but the work has superior breadth and depth. Contains 7,500 signed articles, many with bibliographies, covering all persons, places, objects, customs, and historical events and major teachings of the Bible. KJV, RSV, and ASV are all used. Excellent, but expensive.

7-027     *Theologisches Begriffslexikon zum New Testament.* Coenen, L., E. Beyreuther, and H. Bietenhard (eds.). Brockhaus, 1965-1971. 3 vols. Similar to Kittel, though on a much smaller scale. Conservative (by German standards). Articles follow the alphabetical order of the German, not Greek, works. For English edition, see **7-013** above.

# CHAPTER 8

# Commentaries

From the Latin "commentarius" (annotation), the term "commentary" is generally used in a specific and restrictive sense to refer to a document that analyzes and elucidates a specific biblical text.[1] The text may be very brief (Ralph P. Martin, *Carmen Christi: Philippians 2:5-11 in Recent Interpretation and in the Setting of Early Christian Worship.* Eerdmans, 1983), or a commentary series may treat every book of both testaments as well as the apocrypha (Anchor Bible).

---

[1]Originally, the Latin term *concordantiae* was used to refer to groups of parallel passages. See, Danker, Frederick W. *Multipurpose Tools for Bible Study* (3rd ed. Saint Louis: Concordia Publishing House, 1970), 1 (**2-035**).

In the pre-Christian era the earliest examples of a commentary may be traced to the post-exilic period when oral Aramaic paraphrases of the Hebrew text began to appear. With the appearance of the materials later known as the NT, the early Christians soon developed verse-by-verse comments upon the various books.

Since the acceptance of the historical critical method, commentaries written over the last century and a half have sought to treat the texts in terms of historical setting (date, authorship, purpose), literary character (genre, structure), and philology (syntax and textual reliability).

Commentaries usually print the text being elucidated and upon which commentary is being made.

English language commentaries frequently use the RSV, though older, less reliable versions are sometimes used.

The technical level of the commentaries available varies greatly. Some tend toward inspirational, others focus upon nuances of syntax and vocabulary. Oftentimes, a commentary reflects a specific confessional theology and may portray a particular approach to its task.

But since the advent of biblical criticism the role of the commentary has been defined in even more specific terms: elucidation of text in light of its author, date, recipients, purpose, social and political settings, literary character, and its textual reliability. All of these aspects of study will seldom, if ever, be found in a single commentary, but certain commentaries will stress some aspects while others will go in another direction.

Commentaries often offer great detail in the more subtle nuances of grammar and philology. They can help identify specific words that need further clarification from a good lexicon or other wordbook. They can identify the significant ways in which grammar impinges upon meaning and offer direction about the way these aspects may be pursued.

The purpose here is to list commentaries of varying lengths, from varying confessional traditions, and with a wide variety of technical expertise.

## Single Volume Commentaries

**8-001**      Black, Matthew and Harold Henry Rowley (eds.). *Peake's Commentary on the Bible.* Thomas Nelson and Sons, 1962. This basic commentary contains philological and theological contributions of recent years and is useful for general readers, students, and clergy. This volume has a detailed index and a collection of maps. Supersedes *A Commentary on the Bible*, edited by Arthur S. Peake and Alexander J. Grieve.

**8-002**      Brown, Raymond Edward, Joseph A. Fitzmyer, and Roland Edmund Murphy (eds.). *The Jerome Biblical Commentary.* 2 vols. in 1. Prentice-Hall and Geoffrey Chapman, 1968. A comprehensive work by Catholic scholars containing topical and commentary articles covering the entire Bible, including the apocrypha. Each article contains its own bibliography as well as a bibliography of basic reference works at the end of the book. Designed for students, clergy, laity, and scholars, the general articles in this commentary are particularly valuable in assessing recent trends in scholarship.

**8-003**      Clarke, William Kemp Lowther. *Concise Bible Commentary.* London: SPCK, 1952; Macmillan Company, 1953. Containing valuable introductory essays, this Anglican commentary is divided into five sections dealing with the entire Bible. This work contains an appendix, glossary, full index, courses of study, and extra-canonical literature, including the apocrypha.

**8-004**      Clarke, William Kemp Lowther. *Concise Bible Commentary: Supplement.* SPCK, 1966. Issued to update, expand, and correct material in the original volume (see **8-003**), this is

a valuable adjunct to the basic work and should be used
with it whenever possible.

8-005    Eiselen, Frederick Carl. *The Abingdon Bible Commentary*. Edwin
         Lewis and David George Downey (eds.). Abingdon Press,
         1929 and Epworth Press, 1932. Reprint. Abingdon Press
         and SPCK, 1981. Arranged in five sections covering the
         entire Bible, the introductory articles are valuable, but much
         of the commentary is dated. This commentary does not
         include the apocrypha. The work is ecumenical in its
         selection of contributors. Contains bibliographies, several
         maps, and an index.

8-006    Fuller, R., et. al. *A New Catholic Commentary on Holy Scripture*.
         London: Nelson, 1969. A new revision of the older *A
         Catholic Commentary on Holy Scripture* (1953), this new
         edition is much improved, but not indicative of recent,
         significant Catholic biblical scholarship.

8-007    Laymon, Charles M. (ed.). *The Interpreter's One-Volume
         Commentary on the Bible: Introduction and Commentary
         for Each book of the Bible Including the Apocrypha, with
         General Articles*. Abingdon Press, 1971; London: William
         Collins Publishers, 1972. Intended for use by clergy,
         teachers, and beginning students, this commentary is
         independent of *The Interpreter's Dictionary of the Bible* (7-
         006). General articles by approximately seventy Protestant
         scholars which cover geographical and historical settings,
         biblical languages, money and measures, and chronology
         are brief and nontechnical. Contains many maps, charts,
         illustrations, and subject index.

8-008    Mays, J. L. *Harper's Bible Commentary*. Harper and Row, 1988.
         Intended as a companion volume to *Harper's Bible
         Dictionary* (7-015), it is written in a popular vein and
         contains a narrative commentary which makes use of
         up-to-date scholarship. Completely revised by members of
         the Society for Biblical Literature, this popular commentary
         is widely used. For more extended treatment in the same
         style, see Marsh (8-033). Also published in Britain as *One
         Volume Bible Commentary* (London: Hodder and Stoughton,
         1962).

8-009    Mills, Watson E. and Richard F. Wilson, eds., *Mercer Commentary
         on the Bible*, Mercer University Press, 1994. This one

volume commentary is a companion volume to the *Mercer Dictionary of the Bible* (**7-017**). It contains expositions of all canonical and deutero-canonical books. It is extensively crossed referenced to *MDB*, and contains six general articles.

## Multi-Volume Commentaries

**8-010**     Ackroyd, Peter Runham, A. R. C. Leaney, and J. W. Parker (eds.). *The Cambridge Bible Commentary, New English Bible.* Vol. 1- . Cambridge University Press, 1963- . An ideal tool for the beginner, this series assumes no specialized theological knowledge or understanding of Greek and Hebrew. Seventeen volumes, each containing approximately 200 pages, on the NT were completed in 1967, and works on the OT and Apocrypha are in progress. Useful for both introductory and pastoral studies.

**8-011**     Adeney, Walter Frederic (ed.). *The Century Bible.* 34 vols. Oxford University Press and T. C. and E. C. Jack (1901-1913). Not to be confused with *The New Century Bible* (**8-021**), this series is also referred to as *The New-Century Bible* published by the Caxton Publishing Company. Based on the RV text, it is intended for the general reader and assumes no knowledge of Greek or Hebrew. The brevity on many issues makes it less than useful even at the basic level.

**8-012**     Albright, William Foxwell and David Noel Freedman (eds.). *The Anchor Bible: Introduction, Translation, and Notes.* Vol. 1- . Doubleday and Company, 1964- . Representing both Jewish and Christian scholarship in a new translation with extensive commentary, this series is projected to contain thirty-eight volumes upon completion. Aimed at the general reader but containing several long and detailed analyses, the work would appeal more to the student and specialist requiring quick access to data.

**8-013**     Allen, Clifton J. (ed.). *The Broadman Bible Commentary.* 12 vols. Broadman Press, 1969-1972. Generally intended for general readers and clergy, the articles in this series are not necessarily scholarly or theologically advances. Many of the OT volumes reflect moderate or liberal views, but the NT volumes are more conservative and were written by more traditional scholars.

**8-014**        Barclay, William. *The Daily Bible Study*. Rev. ed. 18 vols.
                 Westminster Press, 1975-1978. Presbyterian in tone, this
                 commentary has special value to the layman and general
                 reader as a guide to the Bible. It includes translation,
                 introduction, and interpretation for the entire Bible; the
                 index is the last volume.

**8-015**        Bowdle, Donald N. *Ellicott's Bible Commentary: A Verse-by-Verse
                 Explanation*. Zondervan Publishing House, 1971. This is a
                 condensation of the eight volume work by Ellicott entitled
                 *A Bible Commentary for English Readers* (**8-025**) and
                 includes modernized language and some reliance on modern
                 scholarship.

**8-016**        Buttrick, George Arthur, et al. (eds.). *The Interpreter's Bible: The
                 Holy Scriptures in the King James and Revised Standard
                 Versions with General Articles and Introduction, Exegesis,
                 Exposition for Each Book of the Bible*. 12 vols. Abingdon
                 Press, 1952-1957. Actually designed for parish ministers,
                 this 12 volume set contains contributions from 125
                 Protestant scholars. It is one of the most complete and most
                 widely respected commentaries published in the twentieth
                 century. Designed to bridge the gap between critical
                 philology and practical application, the double commentary
                 first outlines the exegesis of a passage and then suggests
                 applications. This material is presented on the lower half of
                 each page, while both AV and RSV texts are printed in
                 parallel columns at the top. There are long introductions
                 and helpful bibliographies, indices of subjects and texts.
                 The final volume contains essays on transmission of the
                 NT, the Dead Sea scrolls, and related topics. Generally the
                 introductions, exegesis, and articles are the strongest parts
                 of the work; the didactic and illustrative material in the
                 expository sections is dated and too verbose to be helpful.
                 For a single volume condensation, see Laymon (**8-007**).
                 This is a useful set for church school teachers and
                 beginning students; it is of marginal value in homiletical
                 preparation.

**8-017**        Calvin, Jean. *Calvin's Commentaries*. 45 vols. Edinburgh: Printed
                 for the Calvin Translation Society, 1844-1856. Reprint.
                 Eerdmans, 1948-1959. Volumes in this classic Reformed
                 series are by a number of different translators and are
                 useful for their insights into the history of Protestant
                 biblical interpretation or biblical theology rather than from

an exegetical standpoint. For a new edition of the NT volumes, see the series edited by Torrance & Torrance (**8-018**).

8-018          Calvin, Jean. *Commentaries*. David Wishart Torrance and Thomas Forsyth Torrance (eds.). 12 vols. Oliver and Boyd, 1959-1972 and Eerdmans, 1960-1972. Fulfilling the same purpose as the earlier series on the entire Bible (see **8-017**), these volumes are limited to the NT. This set of translations by various scholars is particularly clear and lucid, conveying the full meaning of Calvin's original text. The series covers the gospels, Pauline epistles and also includes a three-volume harmony.

8-019          Carter, Charles Webb, Ralph Earle, and W. Ralph Thompson (eds.). *The Wesleyan Bible Commentary*. 7 vols. Eerdmans, 1964-1969. Popular in the Wesleyan tradition, this commentary draws on the input of scholars from nine different groups and emphasizes moderate, traditional Protestant views. Focusing on exposition and homiletics rather than scholarship, this series exhibits wide knowledge of secondary literature. Exposition is by paragraph of the biblical test and includes cross-references and bibliographies. Considered to be one of the better Protestant multi-volume commentaries and slightly less objective than Buttrick (**8-016**).

8-020          Clarke, Adam. *The Holy Bible, with Commentary and Critical Notes*. 8 vols. J. Butterworth and Son, 1810-1826. Reprinted as a six-volume set in 1851, it has also been edited in a single volume condensation by Ralph Earle as *Adam Clark's Commentary on the Holy Bible* (Kansas City, MO: Beacon Hill Press of Kansas City, 1967). A classic conservative work which continues to be used in some circles primarily as an expository guide.

8-021          Clements, Ronald E. and Matthew Black (eds.). *The New Century Bible*. Vol. 1- . Oliphants (Marshall, Morgan, and Scott), 1967- . Occasionally cited as *The Century Bible, New Series* (initially published by Thomas Nelson and Sons) to distinguish is from *The Century Bible* (**8-011**), this series is intended to replace the earlier work. Based on the RSV, each volume makes use of the latest critical source materials and exhibits wide knowledge of current scholarly opinion. Nontechnical and clearly written for the less advanced user, the series includes commentaries by several noted Protestant evangelical scholars which would indicate that the overall tone may be slightly biased in the evangelical direction. Upon completion, this commentary will form a useful set of reference works for basic inquiries.

8-022      Davidson, Francis (ed.). *The New Bible Commentary.* Assisted by Alan M. Stibbs and Ernest F. Kevan. 2nd ed. Eerdmans and Intervarsity Fellowship, 1954. Reprint. Eerdmans, 1963. A conservative guide consisting of twelve introductory articles on authority, revelations, and similar topics followed by 66 commentaries, this series is based on the KJV. Belief in divine inspiration underlies all of the commentary, which is not particularly thorough nor acquainted with the results of recent Protestant scholarship. There are appendices treating such topics as the documentary hypothesis from a more or less fundamentalist viewpoint.

8-023      Driver, Samuel Rolles, Alfred Plummer, and Charles Augustus Briggs (eds.). *International Critical Commentary on the Holy Scriptures of the Old and New Testaments.* 45 vols. Charles Scribner's Sons and T. & T. Clark, 1949-1959. This signal series written by British and American scholars consists of volumes on all books of the Bible (some of which are combined into a single volume). Intended to rival the best German scholarship, the ICC charged its contributing editors to incorporate and to discuss in detail the archaeological, philological, historical, and hermeneutical evidence available. This series has withstood the test of time. Overall, the series is highly respected as a useful and often authoritative exegetical guide with strong philological content although the works vary greatly in quality and theological viewpoint as well as in date. Homiletical issues are avoided and the contents are strictly scholarly and analytical. Each volume is well indexed and includes a bibliography of other important works.

8-024      Ecole Biblique in Jerusalem. *La Sainte Bible.* 43 vols. Editions du Cerf, 1948-1959. This series includes a scholarly French translation of the text and helpful exegetical notes by a team of Roman Catholics. Although the approach is detailed and analytical, it reflects the traditional Catholic biblical views of the mid-twentieth century and has been superseded by more recent advances within this tradition. The single volume condensation (Paris: Editions du Cerf, 1956) is very brief but indicative of modern French, Catholic scholarship. The full series is a sound compendium for a relatively advanced audience.

8-025    Ellicott, Charles John (ed.). *A Bible Commentary for English Readers.* 8 vols. Cassell and Company, 1905-1906. Originally published as a 12-volume set in the late nineteenth century (*The Handy Commentary*), this series covers both the OT and the NT in a fairly broad fashion. Less wide-ranging than other works of similar scope and vintage, it has a general background value.

8-026    Erdman, Charles Rosenbury. *Commentary on the New Testament.* 17 vols. Westminster Press, 1916-1936. Reprint. 17 vols. Westminster Press, 1966. A series of brief commentaries which attempts to elucidate the message and outline the contents of each book of the Bible. Some volumes continue to be useful for clergy and general readers although coverage is more expository than exegetical, and much of the commentary is dated. (See also Lenski **8-045**).

8-027    Gaebelein, Frank E. (gen. ed.). *The Expositor's Bible Commentary.* Consulting eds.: Walter C. Kaiser, Jr. et al. Vol. 1- . Zondervan Publishing House, 1976- . A conservative series that provides a collection of comprehensive, scholarly commentaries for exposition and teaching. The first volume contains a collection of pieces on the OT and the NT, general biblical topics and Bible study. An attempt is being made to maintain a balance between philological detail and exposition. The series is more scholarly than Davidson (**8-022**).

8-028    Grant, Frederick Clifton (ed.). *Nelson's Bible Commentary.* 2 vols. Thomas Nelson and Sons, 1962. Based on the RSV, this series appears to be incomplete. Suitable for students, clergy, and advanced general readers, the NT commentaries deal adequately and succinctly with the text. Volume 6 covers Matthew-Acts, and volume 7 covers Romans-Revelation; there are, however, no titles dealing with the OT.

8-029    Hubbard, D. A. *Word Biblical Commentary.* Waco, TX: Word Books, 1982- . Begun in 1977, this series has received wide attention as a moderately technical, yet highly readable, collection. It is aimed at the student, working minister, and others with more specialized interests.

8-030    Kelly, Balmer H. (ed.). *The Layman's Bible Commentary*. 25 vols. John Knox Press, 1959-1964. A series of nontechnical guides based on the RSV and written by Protestant scholars, this commentary is intended to assist the layman in personal study of the Bible and has marginal value in sermon preparation. Although coverage is somewhat uneven, most of the volumes deal clearly and simply with the relevant issues and present utilitarian, if somewhat conservative, analyses of the biblical texts. This version contains Leslie Bullock's 1959 manual, *The Layman's Bible Commentary: A Leader's Guide*, while a British edition, published as *The Layman's Bible Commentaries* (London: SCM Press, 1960-1965), does not.

8-031    Koester, Helmut, et al. (eds.). *Hermeneia: A Critical and Historical Commentary on the Bible*. Vol. 1- . Fortress Press, 1971- . With international and ecumenical contributors, this series, prepared under Lutheran auspices, continues the best tradition of critical and historical scholarship. Intended for the advanced student and scholar, some volumes are English translations of recent commentaries in other languages; all are detailed scholarly works. Coverage extends to the entire Bible, though publication is not yet complete.

8-032    Lock, Walther and David Capell Simpson (eds.). *Westminster Commentaries*. Vol. 1- . Metheun and Company, 1899- . This example of superior scholarship and valuable exposition is one of the few Anglo-Catholic commentaries. It attempts to combine critical principles with clear articulation of the Catholic faith. Each volume includes an introduction and notes on the text of the RV.

8-033    Marsh, John, David M. Paton, and Alan Richardson (gen. eds.). *Torch Bible Commentaries*. Vol. 1- . SCM Press, 1949- . Intended for the general reader, these short commentaries by scholars from various traditions provide useful access to basic information.

8-034    Nicoll, William Robertson (ed.). *The Expositor's Bible*. 49 vols. New York: A. C. Armstrong and Son, 1888-1905; Hodder and Stoughton, 1892-1900. Reprint. Eerdmans, 1956. A series of expository commentaries combining the views of liberal and conservative scholars and showing how various approaches complement one another. An interesting exercise which still has a place in collections devoted to homiletics and to the comparative study of the Bible.

8-035    Sparks, Hedly Frederick Davis (ed.). *The New Clarendon Bible.* Vol. 1- . Clarendon Press, 1963- . Intended to update and fill gaps in Strong's work entitled *The Clarendon Bible* (**8-036**), this series follows the same plan and form but includes the text on the same page as the commentary. Although confusing to use at times (the series began by using the NEB, but later switched to the RSV), the moderate and fairly broad approach exhibited in most volumes makes the series suitable for less advanced users. See also Moule (**8-049**).

8-036    Strong, Thomas Banks, Herbert Wild, and George Herbert Box (eds.). *The Clarendon Bible.* Clarendon Press, 1922-1936. Intended for students, clergy, and informed laity, the overall aim of this series is to present a constructive view of the books of the Bible and their teachings, utilizing the results of modern scholarship without being controversial. The commentary is sound and moderately presented, although difficult exegetical issues tend to be avoided. The series fulfills much the same purpose as Perowne's *Cambridge Bible* (**8-052**) at a slightly more advanced level. For a more recent series, see *The New Clarendon Bible* (**8-035**).

8-037    Zahn, Theodore von (ed.). *Kommentar zum Neuen Testament.* 18 vols. in 20. A. Deichert, 1903-1926. Detailed and wide ranging in its use of continental scholarship, this series contains rather less critical material than Meyer (**8-060**). For readers of German, it is a useful reference source for discussion of NT topics. There have been further editions of selected volumes through 1930, but the entire series has not been revised.

## New Testament Commentaries

8-038    Alford, Henry. *The Greek Testament with a Critically Revised Text, a Digest of Various Readings, Marginal References to Verbal and Idiomatic Usage, Prolegomena, and a Critical and Exegetical Commentary.* Rev. by Everett F. Harrison, 4 vols. in 2. Moody Press, 1958. based on the 1894 edition, this standard nineteenth century Anglican commentary, which includes notes on more difficult passages, does not make use of recent scholarship. Volume 1 covers the gospels and Acts to Corinthians; volume 2 covers the remainder of the NT. Contains some bibliographies. See also Nicoll (**8-050**).

8-039    Bonnard, Pierre, et al. *Commentaire due Nouveau Testament*. Vol. 1- . Editions Delachaux et Niestlé, 1949- . Detailed and clearly written, this series was produced under the auspices of the University de Strasbourg's Protestant theological faculty. While uneven in quality, the articles are thorough and show a wide knowledge of recent advances in biblical scholarship, especially that of continental Protestantism.

8-040    Bruce, Frederick Fyvie (ed.). *The New International Commentary on the New Testament*. Vol. 1- . Eerdmans, 1951- . Until 1962, this series was edited by Ned B. Stonehouse and was called *The New London Commentary on the New Testament* (London: Marshall, Morgan and Scott). Suitable for use by students with a basic grasp of biblical principles, this conservative Protestant series is relatively detailed and exhibits an awareness of recent conservative scholarship.

8-041    *Cambridge Greek Testament for Schools and Colleges*. 19 vols. Cambridge University Press, 1881-1914. Complementing the *Cambridge Bible* (**8-052**), this series includes introductions, maps, and brief notes on words and phrases of the Greek NT. Recent scholarly advances have made many of the volumes rather dated. For a replacement series, see Moule (**8-049**).

8-042    Chadwick, Henry (ed.). *Harper's New Testament Commentaries*. Vol. 1- . Harper and Row, 1957- . Ranging across the full spectrum of critical opinion and providing original translations of the biblical text, this series falls between detailed philological analysis and popular interpretation. Each volume or book of the Bible includes an introduction, translation, and commentary. Very useful for students and clergy, as well as for others looking for quick references on books of the Bible, especially since knowledge of Greek is not necessary. Published simultaneously as *Black's New Testament Gommentaries* (London: A. and C. Black, 1957- ).

8-043    Hendriksen, William. *New Testament Commentary*. 12 vols. Baker Book House, 1980. Adequate as a basic reference tool, each

NT book has an introduction, author's translation of the text, summary, notes, and bibliography.

8-044    Howley, George Cecil Douglas (gen. ed.). *A New Testament Commentary, Based on the Revised Standard Version.* Consulting eds.: Frederick Fyvie Bruce and Henry Leopold Ellison. Zondervan, Pickering and Inglish, 1969. This scholarly, but nontechnical, work by a group of evangelical Protestants, is suitable for beginning students who prefer a conservative approach and require only general information. Commentaries on each book are brief and easy to understand, and cover a wide range of general topics. Contains selective bibliographies. See Tasker (**8-054**) for a more detailed analysis using the same approach.

8-045    Lenski, Richard Charles Henry. *Interpretation of the New Testament.* 11 vols. Columbus, OH: Lutheran Book Concern, 1932. Reprint. 12 vols. Augsburg Publishing House, 1933-1946. Though slightly dated, this Lutheran series is accurate and exhaustive in its interpretation. Includes background information and covers both exegesis of the Greek text and comparison of other commentaries. See also Erdman (**8-026**); for a newer Lutheran series, see Koester (**8-030**).

8-046    Metzger, Bruce Manning. *A Textual Commentary on the Greek New Testament: A Companion Volume to the United Bible Societies' "Greek New Testament".* 3rd ed. United Bible Societies, 1971. Used in conjunction with the standard translation to which it is geared, this commentary provides the rationale for all textual decisions and is particularly valuable in the study of text-critical problems. See also Moule (**8-049**).

8-047    Meyer, Heinrich August Wilhelm (ed.). *Critical and Exegetical Commentary on the New Testament.* Trans. rev. and ed. by W. P. Dickson, W. Stewart and F. Crombie. 20 vols. T. & T. Clark, 1873-1883. A series for more advanced inquiries, this translation of the first German edition of Meyer's critical and exegetical handbooks blends exegesis and theology in the narrative, paying close attention to important critical detail.

8-048    Moffatt, James (ed.). *The Moffatt New Testament Commentary.* 17 vols. Harper and Brothers and Hodder and Stoughton,

1926-1950. Although many noted scholars have contributed to this series by providing a sound commentary on the Moffatt translation, some critics regard the treatment as facile and rather shallow. Based on Moffatt's *New Translation of the Bible*, this work is intended to illuminate the religious meaning and message of the NT and historical and religious issues receive prominent treatment in the narrative commentary. Knowledge of Greek is not required for use of this work.

8-049     Moule, Charles Francis Digby (gen. ed.). *The Cambridge Greek Testament Commentary*. Cambridge University Press, 1955- . Giving special attention to the theological and religious content of the NT in the context of life and worship in Christian communities, this series was designed to supersede the *Cambridge Greek Testament for Schools and Colleges* **(8-041)**. Detailed, but nontechnical, it is designed for users beyond the beginning stages of study. See also *The New Clarendon Bible* **(8-035)** and Metzger **(8-045)**.

8-050     Nicoll, William Robertson (ed.). *The Expositor's Greek Testament*. 5 vols. Dod, Mead, and Company and Hodder and Stoughton, 1897-1910. Reprint. Eerdmans, 1974. Although it is dated, this commentary continues to provide some useful insights into exegesis of the NT epistles in particular. It should be used in conjunction with new works. See also Alford **(8-038)**.

8-051     *The Pelican New Testament Commentaries*. London/Baltimore: Penguin Books, 1963-1969. Each volume in this series provides a full study of each NT book. Coverage extends to religious, historical, critical and linguistic aspects. A useful guide for most levels of inquiry, it is also published as *The Westminster Pelican Commentaries* (Philadelphia, PA: Westminster Press, 1978- ).

8-052     Perowne, John J. Stewart (gen. ed.). *The Cambridge Bible for Schools and Colleges*. 56 vols. Cambridge University Press, 1887-1925. In various editions and with frequent revisions, the series exhibits a sound use of moderate scholarly views and is written in clear, nontechnical language for the nonspecialist. See also the *Cambridge Greek Testament* **(8-041)** and Strong's *Clarendon Bible* **(8-036)**.

8-053      Smyth, Kevin and J. Massyngbaerde (eds.). *Herder's Theological Commentary on the New Testament*. Vol. 1- . Herder and Herder, 1968- . A detailed and thorough Roman Catholic commentary, this excellent translation of the German series by Wilkenhauser and Vögtle (**8-063**) provides a sound reference tool focused on the theological and historical aspects of the NT canon. Each volume includes a bibliography and indices of authors and texts.

8-054      Tasker, Randolph Vincent Greenwood (ed.). *The Tyndale New Testament Commentaries*. 20 vols. Eerdmans and Tyndale House, 1957-1974. Following the KJV text and based on exegesis of the Greek, this series was written by a group of evangelical British and Australian scholars. Reasonably current and scholarly in approach, the volumes are suitable for reference inquiries by beginning students of conservative Protestant background.

## Foreign Language New Testament Commentaries

8-055      Althaus, Paul, H. Appel, O. Bauernfeind, et al. *Theologischer Handkommentar zum Neuer Testament mit Text und Paraphrase*. Vol. 1- . A. Deichert, 1928- . With sound insights into the text and valuable data on exegetical, linguistic and textual matters, this detailed and scholarly commentary series is intended for advanced students. Never completed, the series is being produced in a new edition by Fascher (**8-057**).

8-056      Althaus, Paul and Johannes Behm (eds.). *Das Neue Testament Deutsch: Neues Göttinger Bibelwerk*. In Verbindung mit Hermann Wolfgang Beyer, et al. Vol. 1- . Vandenhoeck and Ruprecht, 1951- . Containing titles by eminent scholars which focus particularly on the issues of NT theology rather than on technical or linguistic matters, this revision of the original series is analytical and detailed, providing useful summaries of current theological thinking on NT texts. Each volume contains a bibliography. For a Roman Catholic counterpart, see Tillmann (**8-062**).

8-057      *Evangelisch-Katholischer Kommentar zum Neuen Testament*. Einsiedeln: Benziger, 1961- . A scholarly ecumenical series utilizing the expertise of noted NT scholars. Each work is intended to illuminate the NT relevance of the OT, to reflect a sound pastoral orientation and to incorporate the insights of contemporary exegesis. Covering the entire NT, this is an excellent series for scholarly inquiries, particularly those who want to compare the insights of modern Protestant and Catholic exegesis.

8-058    Fascher, Erich (ed.). *Theologischer Handkommentar zum Neuen Testamente*. Berlin: Evangelische Verlagsanstal. Intended to supersede the original but incomplete series edited by Althaus (**8-054**), this is an important collection for advanced students. It attempts to interpret the NT *theologically*. These detailed commentaries reflect wide scholarly knowledge. Conservative but open to critical methodology.

8-059    Lietzmann, Hans (ed.). *Handbuch zum Neuen Testament*. In Verbindung mit W. Bauer, Martin Dibelius, et al. 2. Aufl. Vol. 1- . J. C. B. Mohr (Paul Siebeck), 1912- . Although this series is not yet complete, some volumes are very dated, whereas others reflect the present state of continental Protestant criticism reasonably accurately. This commentary series includes the text of the NT as well as complementary volumes on grammar, the apostolic fathers as commentators and other subjects not often found in such undertakings. The commentaries in the second edition of a still incomplete series, originally begun in 1909, are detailed and analytical, reflecting a high degree of exegetical understanding.

8-060    Meyer, Heinrich August Wilhelm (ed.). *Kritisch-Exegetischer Kommentar über das Neuen Testament*. 20 vols. Rev. ed. Vandenhoeck und Ruprecht, 1898-1913. Most volumes are extremely thorough and detailed, but often difficult to comprehend for stylistic reasons. This series has been under revision by various editors since 1930, but many of the later volumes are only reprints of the first or revised edition.

8-061    Strack, Hermann Lebrecht and Paul Billerbeck. *Kommentar zum Neuen Testament aus Talmud und Midrash*. 4 Aufl. 6 vols. Beck, 1965-1969. This collection, written entirely by Billerbeck, follows the canonical order of the NT verse by verse, giving talmudic and midrashic parallel texts and commentaries. Volume 1 deals with Matthew; volume 2, with the other synoptics and apostolic literature; volume 3, with the NT letters. The final two volumes contain a full rabbinic index and a geographical index. This is an excellent series for advanced students and scholars. It has no counterpart.

8-062     Tillmann, Fritz (ed.). *Die Heilige Schrift des Neuen Testamentes.* 10 vols. P. Hanstein, 1931-1950. This series presents a substantial Roman Catholic commentary by continental scholars on the entire Bible. Bibliographies are included but focus primarily on earlier Roman Catholic works. For a more satisfactory and less dated series, see Wikenhauser (**8-064**).

8-063     Wikenhauser, Alfred and Otto Kuss (eds.). *Regensburger Neues Testament.* In Verbindung mit Joseph Freuendorfer, et al. 2 Aufl. Bd. 1- . Verlag Friedrich Pustet, 1966- . Initially begun in 1938 as *Das Neue Testament Übersetzt und Erklärt*, this edition aims to replace Wikenhauser's *Herder's Theologischer Kommentar* (**8-064**). This series is scholarly but relatively traditional in its approach and does not display the same range of Roman Catholic views as does the work by Herder.

8-064     Wikenhauser, Alfred and Anton Vögtle (eds.). *Herder's Theologischer Kommentar zum Neuen Testament.* 2 Aufl. Bd. 1- .; Herder, 1964- . Projected in fourteen volumes with an English translation prepared by Smyth (**8-053**), this series is based on the earlier work by Wikenhauser and Kuss (**8-063**). It is Roman Catholic in origin but ecumenical in content, focusing on the theology and history of the NT canon. The contents of each volume are detailed and are well indexed for advanced reference work. The first edition was begun in 1953 and exhibits a less ecumenical approach to understanding the NT text.

# CHAPTER 9

# Archaeology and Geography

Great strides have been made in the utilization of archaeology as a tool to clarify the understanding of specific biblical texts. Archaeologists can also provide insight into the cultural and historical backgrounds of the various writings. With the advent of new technologies and the use of computer enhancements, this work is becoming more and more efficient in the meticulous identifying, cataloguing, and disseminating work done in the field.

This chapter will list and briefly describe works of general interest to the student of NT archaeology as well as atlases for the location of specific sites.

**9-001**      Ahroni, Jochanan. *Macmillan Bible Atlas*. Rev. ed. New York: Macmillan, 1977. Considered by many scholars to be the best Bible atlas in use today, it has 262 color maps with keys according to books of the Bible, a comparative chronology of early civilizations, and a comprehensive index listing names and places cited in the maps and text. Information in this volume comes from source materials in the fields of Egyptian, Assyrian, Greek, and Roman studies, as well as the Bible.

**9-002**      Albright, William F. *The Archaeology of Palestine*. Rev. ed. by W. G. Dever. Gloucester, MA: Peter Smith, 1976. This volume was first published in 1949 and then revised in 1960 so as to include references to the Qumran discoveries. Covers the various sites by placing their significance into the various periods from the Old Stone Age to the time of the NT.

**9-003**      Albright, William F. *Archaeology and the Religion of Israel*. 5th ed. Baltimore: Johns Hopkins, 1968. First published in 1942 and slightly revised in the several subsequent editions, this volume has been a standard in the field for decades. Although in need of updating, the work is still of considerable value. Covers the premonarchic and monarchic religion of Israel.

**9-004**      Avigad, N. *Discovering Jerusalem*. Nashville: Nelson, 1983. Avigad reports on his excavation of the Jewish Quarter in Jerusalem. Clearly written, very informative, amply illustrated.

**9-005**      Baly, Dennis. *Geographical Companion to the Bible*. New York: McGraw-Hill, 1963. Supplements Baly's *Geography* (**9-006**) by giving interesting background information about battlefields, trade routes, city life, etc. Very readable. Indicates how the study of archaeology is inextricably tied to the study of the biblical documents.

**9-006**      Baly, Dennis. *The Geography of the Bible*. 2nd ed. New York: Harper, 1974. Covers thoroughly the geology, meteorology, and physical geography of the regions of Israel. Very detailed information.

**9-007**      Baly, Dennis and A. D. Tushingham. *Atlas of the Biblical World*. New York: World, 1971. Designed to produce a better understanding of the Biblical environment, this volume contains 49 maps and many illustrations. Also contains an excellent bibliography and indices to the text.

9-008      Dever, W. G. and H. D. Lance. *A Manual of Field Excavation: Handbook for Field Archaeologists.* Cincinnati: Israel Exploration Society, 1978. This volume documents the specific procedures used in the field. It covers the principles of excavation, of archaeological photography, of field recording. It describes tools and equipment used on the dig.

9-009      Finegan, Jack. *Light from the Ancient Past.* 2nd ed. Princeton: Princeton University Press, 1969. An excellent introductory volume for the beginner. Covers in broad strokes the background of early Christianity. Details the archaeological work done in Palestine as it relates to understanding the NT.

9-010      Grollenberg, Lucas Henricus. *Atlas of the Bible.* Translated and edited by Joyce M. H. Reid and H. H. Rowley. London: Nelson, 1956. In addition to many fine maps, the text summarizes Biblical history, arranged chronologically. Contains a full general index, many illustrations of people, land, artifacts, and archaeological discoveries in the Holy Lands.

9-011      Kareling, Emil Gottlieb Henrich. *Rand McNally Bible Atlas.* 3d. ed. Chicago: Rand McNally, 1966. Arranged in chronological order, the text, maps, and photos are combined to give a picture of the world in Biblical times. Contains annotated table of contents, geographical index, and subject index.

9-012      Kenyon, K. *The Bible and Recent Archaeology.* Revised by P. Moorey. Louisville, KY: John Knox, 1987. A good source for understanding the relationship between archaeology and the Bible. More attention is given to the OT era, but the Palestine of the NT era is discussed.

9-013      May, Herbert Gordon (ed.). *Oxford Bible Atlas.* 2d ed. New York: Oxford University Press, 1974. This small but handy-sized atlas has 52 pages of maps and offers an introduction on Israel and the Nations, an article on "Archaeology and the Bible," and a gazetteer. Available in paperback.

9-014      Miller, J. Maxwell. *Introducing the Holy Land.* Macon, GA: Mercer University Press, 1985. Written by a veteran traveller to Palestine, this small volume is packed with information, charts, drawings, photos. It is specifically intended for anyone planning a trip to Israel, but includes much information of a general nature.

**9-015**     Monson, J., et al. *Student Map Manual: Historical Geography of the Bible Lands* Grand Rapids: Zondervan, 1979. Consists of numerous maps not only of Israel but also of the Transjordan and parts of Egypt. More than 850 sites are identified by map reference.

**9-016**     Moorey, R. *Excavation in Palestine*. Grand Rapids: Eerdmans, 1981. This easy to read and clearly written introduction to archaeology covers its history, development, and relationship to the Bible. Illustrated.

**9-017**     Murphy-O'Connor, Jerome. *The Holy Land: An Archaeological Guide from Earliest Times to 1700*. 2nd. rev. ed. Oxford: Oxford University Press, 1986. Provides the historical background to the significant biblical sites, with major attention being given to the Jerusalem sites.

**9-018**     Nengenman, Jan H. *New Atlas of the Bible*. Garden City, NY: Doubleday, 1969. Tracing the growth of the Bible in the setting of the history out of which it came, this volume offers concise, clear information on the way the Bible was translated from Greek and Hebrew originals—interpreted, criticized, and most recently illuminated by the findings of modern biblical research and scholarship—while stressing the Bible as the expression of religious vision interacting with human experience. Arranged in chronological order with an alphabetical index in the back, this volume also contains 200 photographs, manuscripts, and reconstructions.

**9-019**     Wright, George Ernest. *Biblical Archaeology*. Rev. ed. Louisville, KY: Westminster, 1962. Arranged in historical sequence from prehistoric to NT times, this volume is the standard in the field.

**9-020**     Wright, George Ernest and Floyd V. Filson. *The Westminster Historical Atlas to the Bible*. Rev. ed. Philadelphia: Westminster Press, 1956. This volume is an atlas as well as a geographical study of the Holy Land in Bible times. All Bible place names are catalogued in the back with their identifications in either a text index, a map index, or an index of Arabic names identified with biblical places in Syria and Palestine.

# CHAPTER 10

# Texts of the New Testament

**10-001**　　Aland, B., K. Aland, J. Karavidopoulos, C. M. Martini, and B. M. Metzger (eds.). *The Greek New Testament.* 4th ed. New York/London/Edinburgh/ Amsterdam/ Stuttgart: United Bible Societies, 1993. This widely used Greek NT was first issued in 1966. The main difference between it and the *Novum Testamentum graece* is seen in the *apparatus criticus*, which has been restricted to the major text-critical problems of the Greek NT. The restriction was made because of the purpose of this edition, being destined for and adapted to the needs of Bible translators throughout the world. Though the evaluative judgment of the committee that worked on the text is generally good, there are times when those judgments have been affected by long-standing scholarly prejudices (e.g., the so-called Western non-interpolations in the last chapters of the Lucan Gospel).

**10-002**　　Bover, J. M. *Novi Testamenti biblia graeca et latina.* 5th ed. Madrid: Consejo superior de investigaciones científicas,

1968. A resultant text based on the agreements of six main critical editions with added information derived from Merk and the works of Jacquier, A. C. Clark, and Allo. Much detailed data is included when readings are mentioned and variants are adopted which, in Bover's opinion, are supported by the testimony of the most ancient and best codices, versions and ecclesiastical writers.

10-003    Bover, J. M. and J. O'Callaghan. *Nuevo Testamento trilingüe*. BAC 400; Madris: La editorial católica, 1977. The Greek text of the NT is flanked by that of the Latin Vulgate; beneath them is Bover's latest Spanish translation. An *apparatus criticus* accompanies both the Greek and Latin texts; occasional brief notes explain the Spanish translation. The *apparatus* adds witnesses from all the papyri; the introduction offers a Spanish translation of the majority of Bover's Latin prolegomena.

10-004    Kilpatrick, G. D. (ed.). *Hē kainē diathēkē*. 2d ed. London: British and Foreign Bible Society, 1958. First published in 1954, this text is based on Eberhard Nestle's text of 1904; its *apparatus criticus* was prepared by Kilpatrick with the aid of Erwin Nestle and others. The text of 1904 was changed in only 11 places; the *apparatus* is not as abundant as that of Nestle, but a thoroughgoing eclecticism dominates the use of manuscript evidence in the *apparatus*.

10-005    Legg, S. C. E. *Novum Testamentum graece secundum textum Westcotto-Hortianum: Evangelium secundum Marcum cum aparatu critico novo plenissimo, lectionibus codicum nuper reportorum additis, editionibus versionum antiquarum et patrum ecclesiasticorum denuo investigatis*. Oxford: Clarendon, 1935. This ambitions project was begun over 60 years ago. Legg published texts of Mark (1935) and Matthew (1940). This project was severely criticized. Generally, it was thought to be much too ambitious for a single scholar.

10-006    Merk, A. *Novum Testamentum graece et latine*. 9th ed. Rome: Biblical Institute, 1964. Based on von Soden's text I when first published in 1933, the present editions offer an eclectic text based on the evidence of manuscripts, ancient versions, readings in ecclesiastical writers, and critical studies. Contains useful appendix giving variants in recently discovered papyri.

10-007    Nestle, E., et al. *Novum Testamentum graece.* 26th Rev. ed. by K. and B. Aland assisted by M. Black, C. Martini, B. Metzger and A. Wikgren. Stuttgart: Deutsche Bibelstifung; London: United Bible Societies, 1981. A widely-used pocket edition, this volume was first published in 1898. Aimed at constructing a text based not on personal opinions but on the critical editions of Tischendorf and Westcott-Hort, editions from 1927 on also contain evidence from manuscript witnesses as well. Contains compact *apparatus criticus* being vastly superior, i.e., quite detailed and based on readings in manuscripts (papyri, uncials, and minuscules), versions, patristic writings, and lectionaries. The introduction contains useful technical information; the appendices list the Greek and Latin manuscripts used in the preparation of this edition; also contains a list of sigla and abbreviations.

10-008    Soden, H. von. *Die Schriften des Neuen Testaments in ihrer ältesten erreichbaren Textgestalt hergestellt auf Grund ihrer Textgeschichte.* 2nd ed. 2 vols. Göttingen: Vandenhoeck & Ruprecht, 1911, 1913. Although old, and many scholars disagree with the principles upon which the con Soden text is often based, this edition is still useful.

10-009    Tischendorf, C. *Novum Testamentum graece.* 2 vols.; 8th ed. Leipzig: Giescke und Devrient, 1869, 1872. This work contains a thorough *apparatus criticus* that is helpful even today for many problems, but many new texts have come to light since 1894.

10-010    Westcott, B. F. and F. J. A. Hort. *The New Testament in the Original Greek.* 2 vols. rev. ed. Cambridge/London: Macmillan 1890-1896. Even though text-critical study has moved far beyond Westcott-Hort, the influence of this edition is still seen in many ways.

# CHAPTER 11

# Grammars

11-001      Blass, F. and A. Debrunner. *Grammatik des neutestamentlichen Griechisch.* 14th ed; rev. F. Rehkopf. Vandenhoeck & Ruprecht, 1976. Long the standard Greek reference grammar for studying the NT, R. W. Funk has established the same reputation in the English speaking world for the translation and revision of this work. Awkward to use; the user is required to check two or three places in any paragraph entry to find all relevant material. Even with format problems, Blass-Debrunner-Funk is a recognized authority.

11-002      Burton, E. DeW. *Syntax of the Moods and Tenses of New Testament Greek.* 3rd ed. Seabury, 1898/1976. This work is not a full-fledged reference grammar, but it is the last word in comprehending and classifying NT verbs. In almost a century there has been nothing to match it.

**11-003**   Chamberlain, W. D. *An Exegetical Grammar of the Greek New Testament.* Baker, 1941/1975. A paperback reprint of a classic title, this work represents the intermediate step between Davis and Robertson's large reference grammar. Chamberlain uses the eight-case division for nouns. Chamberlain was a student of A. T. Robertson, one of the great names in NT philology.

**11-004**   Dana, H. E. and J. R. Mantey. *A Manual Grammar of the Greek New Testament.* Macmillan, 1927/1957. A one-volume intermediate grammar with a sensible arrangement and numerous examples. Greeks texts cited to illustrate a point are translated on the spot, something an intermediate student will welcome.

**11-005**   David, W. H. *Beginner's Grammar of the Greek New Testament.* Harper & Row, 1923. Also a student of Robertson's (see Chamberlain, **11-003**), Davis designed this work to bring those with no knowledge of Greek up to a level where they could use Robertson's more sophisticated grammars. Ordinarily unimportant but for the fact that Robertson and his students insisted on distinguishing eight cases for the Greek noun, while all others use five. The user should know, however, that the eight-case distinction is no longer accepted.

**11-006**   Gignac, F. T. *A Grammar of the Greek Papyri of the Roman and Byzantine Periods.* Testi e documenti per lo studio dell'antichità, 55. 4 vols. Istituto editoriale cisalpino, La Goliardica: 1976, 1981. These volumes of the important grammar of the non-literary Greek papyri from Roman and Byzantine Egypt are divided as follows: volume 1 treats the phonology of these texts; volume 2 treat their morphology; volumes 3 and 4 treat their syntax. Approximately 32,300 documents have been analyzed in this preparation of this work.

**11-007**   LaSor, W. S. *Handbook of New Testament Greek: An Inductive Approach Based on the Greek Text of Acts.* 2 vols. Eerdmans, 1973. Using the inductive approach, the student starts out with the briefest introduction and begins quickly to read Acts under LaSor's guidance, building a knowledge of grammar as the reading progresses.

11-008    Machen, J. G. *New Testament Greek for Beginners*. Macmillan, 1923. So well done almost sixty years ago, this original edition may be the all-time favorite introductory grammar for the NT Greek. Not well-suited for self-instruction though.

11-009    Mayser, E. *Grammatik der griechischen Papyri aus der Ptolemäerzeit: Mit Einschluss der gleichzeitigen Ostraka und der in Ägypten verfassten Inschriften*. 2nd ed. de Gruyter, n.d. This unfinished work constitutes a partial reference grammar of Greek non-literary writings of the Ptolemaic and early Roman periods of Egypt inscribed in papyrus, potsherds, and stone monuments.

11-010    Moule, C. F. D. *An Idiom Book of New Testament Greek*. 2nd ed. Cambridge University Press, 1959. Not a reference grammar of the usual sort, this compact survey concentrates on the major characteristics of NT Greek. It highlights most of the difficult phrases and ambiguous passages. Available in paperback.

11-011    Moulton, J. H. (ed. H. G. Meecham). *An Introduction to the Study of New Testament Greek*. 5th ed. Macmillan, 1955. Although small, this is a formidable and informative introduction. One of its finest features is a "first reader" at the end, a synthetic set of texts of increasing difficulty. Not the simplest book for self-instruction.

11-012    Moulton, J. H. and F. W. Howard. *A Grammar of the New Testament Greek*. 4 vols. Clark, 1929-1976. Though this grammar was written over a long period of time, it is the best comprehensive reference grammar of NT Greek, even though parts of it would not be as up-to-date as Blass-Debrunner **(11-001)**. A full-fledged reference grammar; concise and well-indexed.

11-013    Robertson, A. T. *A Grammar of the Greek New Testament in the Light of Historical Research*. 4th ed. Broadman, 1923/1934. Written like an extended essay, this is the only advanced grammar that can be read like a book. It is also harder to use for quick reference purposes, but this grammar is the doorway to the history of the Greek language and to a view of the NT from that vantage point.

11-014    Robertson, A. T. and W. H. David. *A New Short Grammar of the Greek New Testament: For Students Familiar with the*

*Elements of Greek.* 10th ed. Baker, 1933. Specifically written as an intermediate grammar, Robertson (a philologist and historian of the Greek language), included much that is not ordinarily found in such efforts. Included are grammatical examples from papyri and inscriptions which make the book meatier than most intermediate grammars and somewhat more sophisticated but at the same time, more difficult to use. It is the richest, if not most efficient, intermediate grammar.

**11-015**     Thackerary, H. St. J. *A Grammar of the Old Testament in Greek according to the Septuagint.* University Press, 1909; reprinted 1978. Despite being outdated, the work remains the one indispensable grammar of the Greek OT.

**11-016**     Zerwick, M. *Analysis philologica Novi Testamenti graeci.* 3d ed. Biblical Institute, 1966. Intended for beginners, this companion volume to Merk's NT Greek text (**10-006**), this work supplies a running lexical and grammatical analysis of the NT words and phrases, together with frequent exegetical comments.

**11-017**     Zerwick, M. *Biblical Greek: English Edition Adapted from the 4th Latin Edition by J. Smith.* Loyola University Press, 1963. Originally written in Latin for seminarians beginning their study of the Greek NT, this English translation is welcome. Zerwick later wrote a grammatical analysis of the entire NT that is keyed to paragraph numbers in this grammar. Thus, when a puzzling turn of grammar comes up in the NT and Zerwick solves the puzzle, he also refers the reader to a larger discussion in this book. A superb tool.

# CHAPTER 12

# Lexicons

**12-001**    Abbott-Smith, G. (ed.). *A Manual Greek Lexicon of the New Testament.* 3rd ed. Greenwood, SC: Attic Press, 1937/1977. Of manageable size, this work has several good features: etymologies, citations of Hebrew words underlying the Septuagint and NT Greek usage, and synonyms. Great for quick, easy reference, and not other lexicon crams so much information into such a small package.

**12-002**    Bailly, A. *Dictionnaire grec français.* Paris: Hachette, 1950. The French counterpart of LSJ, issued between the 9th edition of the latter and its *Supplement.* An appendix supplies useful tables on Greek numbering, coins, names of months, and measurement of length, weight, and capacity. Some reprintings also have a supplement on Greek mythology and religion.

**12-003**    Bauer, W., F. W. Gingrich, and F. W. Danker. *A Greek-English Lexicon of the New Testament and Other Early Christian*

*Literature: A Translation and Adaptation of the Fourth Revised and Augmented Edition of Walter Bauer's Griechisch-Deutsches Wörterbuch zu den Schriften des Neuen Testaments und der übrigen urchristichen Literatur* by William F. Arndt and F. Wilbur Gingrich. 2nd ed. rev. from Bauer's 5th ed. Chicago/ London: University of Chicago, 1979. This second edition utilizes much of the new material that Bauer introduced into his 5th edition and adds some that the present editors have gathered on their own. Use of it over a period of time makes one realize that all is not yet perfect—but much improved as it contains some 20% additional material.

12-004    Berry, G. R. (ed.). *Berry's Greek-English New Testament Lexicon with Synonyms.* Grand Rapids: Baker, 1980. This original paperback is actually a separate reprinting of material found in Berry's interlinear NT. The lexicon is coded to the numbering system of Strong's *Exhaustive Concordance.* The chief virtues of this lexicon are is portability and its usefulness for "Quick Greek."

12-005    Chantraine, P. *Dictionnaire étymologique de la langue grecque: Histoire des motis.* 4 vols. Paris: Klincksieck, 1968, 1970, 1974. Chantraine died in June 1974, having finished just three-fourths of volume 4 (up to *phainmō*); the rest is to be completed by a team of colleagues.

12-006    Cremer, H. *Biblio-Theological Lexicon of New Testament Greek.* 4th ed. Edinburgh: T. & T. Clark, 1895. Though frequently reprinted after the appearance of the fourth edition and badly out-of-date, this work still offers some interesting essays, arranged alphabetically by Greek words.

12-007    Daris, S. *Spoglio lessicale papirologico.* 3 vols. Milan: Istituto di papirologia dell'Università cattolica del Sacro Cuore, 1968. A work intended to update the Preisigke *Wörterbuch* (12-017), but which has to be used with great caution; one must always check the references.

12-008    Frisk, H. *Griechisches etymologisches Wörterbuch.* Indogermanische Bibliothek, II. Reihe; 3 vols. Heidelberg: C. Winter, 1960, 1970, 1972. This and the Chantraine title (12-005) are the two standard etymological dictionaries to which the student may have to turn from time to time, as questions arise about the historical etymology of Greek words.

12-009    Gingrich, F. W. *A Shorter Lexicon of the Greek New Testament.* Chicago: University of Chicago; Grand Rapids: Zondervan, 1957/1965. An abridgement of the first edition of Bauer-Arndt-Gingrich, this edition confines its listings to the basic meanings of words and to citations from the NT. Textual variants are noted. It is reasonably up-to-date and handy.

12-010    Lampe, G. W. H. (ed.). *A Patristic Greek Lexicon.* New York: Oxford, 1961/1968. This huge volume catalogues the Greek vocabulary of the early church. Highly technical, definitive, and expensive.

12-011    Liddell, H. G. and R. Scott (eds.). *Abridged Greek-English Lexicon.* New York: Oxford, 1953. Still briefer than either of the other editions (see **12-012** and **12-013**). Designed for classroom use.

12-012    Liddell, H. G. and R. Scott. *A Greek-English Lexicon: A New Edition Revised and Augmented Throughout.* 9th ed. 2 vols. Oxford: Clarendon, 1925-1940; reprinted 1966. New edition, rev. by H. A. Jones, with a supplement by E. A. Barber. New York: Oxford, 1968. Mainly devoted to classical Greek, this excellent lexicon frequently includes references to the LXX and the NT. Especially useful for tracing the early history of a NT word or for determining its etymology. The standard in Greek dictionaries.

12-013    Liddell, H. G. and R. Scott (eds.). *Intermediate Greek-English Lexicon.* New York: Oxford, 1889/1957. A considerable abridgment of *A Greek-English Lexicon* (see **12-012**). Easy to use for quick reference, but not definitive.

12-014    Moulton, H. K. *The Analytical Greek-English Lexicon Revised.* Grand Rapids: Zondervan, 1978. An updated version of a much older lexicon, it lists alphabetically every form of every NT word. The emphasis in such "analytical lexicons" is not just on the meaning of the Greek words but also on recognizing the specific form of each. "Quick Greek" is designed for the beginner.

12-015    Moulton, J. H. and G. Milligan. *The Vocabulary of the Greek Testament, Illustrated from the Papyri and Other*

*Non-Literary Sources.* 2d ed. London: Hodder and Stoughton, 1957. Not a complete lexicon of the NT, this work lists only those Greek words of NT vocabulary which are found in non-literary papyri and other non-literary sources (i.e., inscriptions, etc.). A technical and specialized tool.

**12-016**     Newman, B. M. *A Concise Greek-English Dictionary of the New Testament.* New York: American Bible Society/London: United Bible Societies, 1971. This brief lexicon is available separately or bound with the UBS Greek NT for which it was designed to be used. Maps indicate place names; irregular verbs are cited alphabetically and according to their proper primary form.

**12-017**     Preisigke, F. *Wörterbuch der griechischen Papyrusurkunden mit Einschluss der griechischen Inschriften Aufschriften Ostraka Mumienschilder usw. aus Ägypten.* 3 vols. Berlin: Privately published, 1925, 1927, 1931. A very important comprehensive dictionary of non-literary Greek texts found in papyri and inscriptions from Egypt. Though dated, it is still an indispensable tool for a thorough study of NT Greek.

**12-018**     Schleusner, J. F. *Novus Thesaurus philologico-criticus: sive, Lexicon in LXX. et reliquos interpretes graecos ac scriptores apochrphos Veteris Testamenti.* 3 vols. London: J. Duncan, 1829. This remains the only lexicon of the Greek OT in existence. Though it retains some value, students will most often do better to refer to one of the several modern lexicons of NT Greek.

**12-019**     Sophocles, E. A. *Greek Lexicon of the Roman and Byzantine Periods (from BC 146–AD 1100).* Rev. ed. New York: Scribner's, 1887; reprinted, 1957. An old, not carefully constructed, lexicon which may still help in certain problems, where no other lexicons cover the same matter.

**12-020**     Souter, A. (ed.). *Pocket Lexicon to the Greek New Testament.* New York: Oxford University Press, 1916. An old favorite that is handy and compact, Souter remains in demand because so much reliable information is compressed into fewer than 300 pages. Although not as up-to-date, this is a clear alternative to the abridged version of Bauer-Arndt-Gingrich (**12-003**).

12-021    Thayer, J. H. *Greek-English Lexicon of the New Testament.* Grand
          Rapids: Zondervan, 1889/1956. First appearing in
          1885-1886 as a translation of a German effort (the
          Grimm-Wilde *Clavis*), Thayer's work was revised a few
          years later and became the standard NT lexicon until the
          appearance of the first edition of Bauer-Arndt-Gingrich (**12-
          003**). Thayer remains popular and can be found in a variety
          of new editions. For example, *Thayer's Greek-English
          Lexicon of the New Testament.* Grand Rapids: Baker
          (1889/n.d.). Paperback edition keyed to the numerical code
          of Strong's *Exhaustive Concordance* (**13-020**). Good for
          "Quick Greek." Alos published as *Thayer's Greek-English
          Lexicon of the New Testament.* Nashville: Broadman,
          1889/1978. Paperback.

12-022    Zorell, F. *Lexicon graecum Novi Testamenti.* 3rd ed. Cursus sacrae
          Scripturae, pars prior, libri introductorii, 7. Paris:
          Leithielleux, 1961. When it was first published in 1911, this
          lexicon was the only NT lexicon which had made use of the
          material coming from the papyri. It is a lexicon of the
          canonical NT writings only. The second and third editions
          make use of the research of Preuschen, Bauer, Preisigke,
          Moulton, Milligan, and have added a "supplementum
          bibliographicum" of 40 pages. It has not been kept
          up-to-date but is still useful in many ways.

# CHAPTER 13

# Concordances

A concordance is a compilation of all of the words that appear in any given Bible text. The entries are arranged first alphabetically by each word entered, and secondly by biblical book under each word. Thus, under "Tychicus" one would find this entry (in Young's *Concordance* [13-025]):

TY-CHI´-CHUS, Τυχικός, *fortunate*.

A believer in Asia Minor, who accompanied Paul to Jerusalem, when he left Greece and was sent by him first to Ephesus, and then to Colosse.

Acts 20:4      there accompanied him . . . T

Eph 6:21      T . . . shall make known to you all things

Col 4:7        All my state shall T. declare unto you

2 Tim 4:12     And T. have I sent to Ephesus

Titus 3:12     I shall send Artemas unto thee, or T.


Essentially, then, a concordance indicates how many times a given term occurs in the text upon which the specific concordance is based. Of course, there are other uses beyond this obvious one, though it is precisely this functional aspect from which the "concordance" takes it name.[1]

Concordances have been around for along time,[2] but have become very popular and widely used since the publication of *Nelson's Complete Concordance of the Revised Standard Version Bible* (**13-006**) in 1957. The relative cost of obtaining a good, usable concordance has steadily decreased.


**13-001**     Aland, K., et al. (eds.). *Volständige Kondorkanz zum grieschischen NT*. 2 vols. Berlin: de Gruyter, 1975-1982. A definitive concordance, this work gives longer lemmata than most. Up-to-date textual data. Vol. II (1978) gives full statistical data on distribution of vocabulary, frequency of word-forms, hapax legomena, etc.

**13-002**     Bachmann, H. and W. A. Slaby. *Computer Konkordanz zum novum testamentum Graece von Nestle Aland 26. Auflage, und zum Greek New Testament*. New York: de Gruyter, 1980. 3rd ed. Simply referred to in English as the ''Computer

---

[1]Originally, the Latin term *concordantiae* was used to refer to groups of parallel passages. See Frederick W. Danker, *Multipurpose Tools for Bible Study* (3rd ed. Saint Louis: Concordia Publishing House, 1970), 1 (**2-035**).

[2]The first might have been the concordance of the Vulgate completed by more than 300 monks in early 13th century.

Concordance," this is the most complete and useful concordance to the Greek NT available today. Technical.

13-003     Cruden, A. (ed.). *Cruden's Unabridged Concordance*. Nashville: Broadman, n.d. After its appearance in 1737, the name Cruden became almost inseparable from the term "concordance." It is still a useful work, but its age and limitations are evident in the face of newer and more sophisticated works. Contains the occurrence of significant words of Scripture (in alphabetical order) and is one of the few concordances that includes the apocryphal books.

13-004     Darton, Michael (ed.). *Modern Concordance to the New Testament*. Garden City, NY: Doubleday, 1975. The ideal concordance for students wishing to study the NT in various modern English translations. Arranged by over 300 concepts or themes with subdivisions, the material contains an English transliteration of the Greek word it covers. Contains an index of English words used in the NT, a Greek word index, an index to proper names, and a list of Greek words.

13-005     Edwards, R. A. *A Concordance to Q*. SBLSBS 7. Atlanta: Scholars Press, 1975. Indices each word in the double tradition of Matthew and Luke (according to the author's reconstruction). It lists all the words in the Q passages, and secondly all the words in each pericope (both in alphabetical order).

13-006     Ellison, John W. *Nelson's Complete Concordance of the Revised Standard Version of the Bible*. New York: Nelson, 1957. Because of the use of the computer in the preparation of this concordance, it is neither analytical nor does it contain the Greek and Hebrew words from which the English words have come. Relatively easy to use with the words listed in alphabetical order and Scripture reference in Biblical order, this work omits certain words. A list of these words is found in the front of the text.

13-007     Gall, J. *Layman's English-Greek Concordance*. Grand Rapids: Baker, 1974. This concordance is brief and less than adequate for serious work. As the title suggests, the listing is by English words.

13-008     Gaston, L. *Horae Synopticae Electronica: Word Statistics of the Synoptic Gospels*. Society of Biblical Literature, 1973. This is an attempt to be more precise with the aid of a computer, taking into account the postulates of form-criticism and more recent views on sources.

13-009    Hartdegen, S. J. (ed.). *Nelson's Complete Concordance of the New American Bible*. Nashville/New York: Nelson, 1977. This is a well-produced concordance of the New American Bible, the national acclaimed Roman Catholic translation of 1970. The publisher sometimes refers to this volume without reference to the editor's name with the title *Nelson's Complete New American Bible Concordance* (**13-006**).

13-010    Hatch, E. and H. Redpath. *A Concordance to the Septuagint and the Older Greek Versions of the Old Testament (Including the Apocryphal Books)*. 2 vols. Oxford: Clarendon Press, 1987. Although drawing upon only four manuscripts, this work is indispensable for the study of the LXX. Most helpful when used together with E. Camilo dos Santos, *An Expanded Hebrew Index for the Hatch-Redpath Concordance of the Septuagint*. Jerusalem: Dugith, 1973. The latter lists all the Greek equivalents next to the Semitic words (in alphabetical order).

13-011    Hawkins, John. *Horae Synopticae: Contributions to the Study of the Synoptic Problem*. 2nd ed. Society of Biblical Literature, 1909. Useful for the synoptic criticism. Contains lists of words and phrases. Again, the WH text is used (**10-010**).

13-012    Jacques, X. *List of New Testament Words Sharing Common Elements: Supplement to Concordance or Dictionary*. Rome: Biblical Institute Press, 1969. This work groups together words from the same root, which in a dictionary or concordance are necessarily separated by alphabetic arrangement. A great help.

13-013    Joy, Charles Rhind. *Harper's Topical Concordance*. Rev. and enl. ed. New York: Harper, 1962. Unlike the regular concordance, this work does not enable one to find a particular verse under the principal words it contains. This work helps one find appropriate texts for topics even though the topic itself is not among the words of the texts. Topics are listed in alphabetical order and the texts are arranged in Biblical order. Only significant and vivid verses are included. Proper names are included only if they have symbolic significance.

**13-014**     Morgenthaler, R. *Statistik der neutestamentlichen Wortschatzes.* Zürich: Gotthelf-Verlag, 1958. Particularly useful for any type of *Vokabelstatistik* work, this volume contains a lengthy introduction and detailed tables giving the occurrences of a word in the different NT books which eliminates a lot of tedious word counting.

**13-015**     Morrison, C. (ed.). *An Analytical Concordance to the Revised Standard Version of the New Testament.* Philadelphia: Westminster, 1979. Covering only the NT, it must be considered the new standard for the most frequently used and cited translation in America today, the RSV NT. Primarily designed for readers who do not know Greek, Morrison offers the Greek word for every English entry. Highly recommended for both technical and popular use.

**13-016**     Moulton, W. F. and A. S. Geden. *A Concordance to the Greek Testament: According to the Texts of Westcott and Hort, Tischendorf, and the English Revisers.* Greenwood, SC: Attic Press, 1978. 5th ed. For generations this work has been the standard Greek NT concordance in English. It remains a basic, reliable technical resource, even though it has been eclipsed.

**13-017**     Schmoller, A. (ed.). *Handkonkordanz zum Neuen Testament.* New York: American Bible Society/Stuttgart: German Bible Society, 1973. 15th ed. While this is not a rival of previous entries for completeness, it is the best compact concordance of the Greek text available. Limited range, but a fine technical tool for scholars; less useful for more general readers.

**13-018**     Smith, J. B. (ed.). *Greek-English Concordance to the New Testament.* Scottdale, PA: Herald Press, 1955. A most helpful tool available in opening up the Greek text for the general reader; less useful to the scholar. The tabular arrangement conveys an enormous amount of information quickly and enables the reader to see, at a glance, the whole range of translations of any particular Greek word and to determine the number of occurrences, book by book, in the NT. Contains English-to-Greek index.

**13-019**     Stagenga, J. *The Greek-English Analytical Concordance of the Greek-English New Testament.* Jackson, MS: Hellenes-English Biblical Foundations, 1963. Based on the *Textus Receptus* (of 1550), this concordance offers Greek words with English translations. Good for "Quick Greek."

**13-020**     Strong, James. *The Exhaustive Concordance of the Bible.* Nashville: Abingdon-Cokesbury, 1980. The most complete concordance, this work contains every word in the KJV of the Bible and all the passages where they are found. Analytical but complete, simple, and accurate.

**13-021**     Wigram, G. V. (ed.). *The Englishman's Greek Concordance of the New Testament.* Grand Rapids: Zondervan, 1883-1889. An old classic admired by those who want to look up words in Greek and find the citations translated into English. Based on older Greek NT editions, it is not up-to-date but it is still popular.

**13-022**     Wigram, G. V. (ed.). *The Englishman's Greek Concordance of the New Testament: Numerically Coded to "Strong's Exhaustive Concordance."* Grand Rapids: Baker, 1883/1980. Same as **13-021**, but in paperback.

**13-023**     Winter, R. D. *The World-Study Concordance.* 9th ed. Wheaton, IL: Tyndale, 1978. Basically the same as the Wigram concordance (**13-021** and **13-022** above), but has a few added extra features here and there. Greek concordance is in alphabetical order with citations following the English of the KJV. For "Quick Greek," this book works like a central switchboard connecting the reader with other major reference works.

**13-024**     Yoder, J. D. *Concordance to the Distinctive Greek Text of Codes Bezae.* NTTS 2. Leiden: Brill, 1961. Useful in the study of this particular manuscript, but has been criticised for omitting the definite article and the post-positive *de*.

**13-025**     Young, Robert. *Analytical Concordance to the Bible on an Entirely New Plan.* 22nd American ed., rev. New York: Funk & Wagnall, 1936. Containing approximately 311,000 references subdivided by reference to the original words in Hebrew and Greek, this work assists the reader in analyzing different shades of meanings of words. Also contains a list of proper names and their pronunciation, an index lexicon to the OT and the NT, and a section dealing with recent discovering in Bible lands.

# CHAPTER 14

# Synopses

14-001    Aland, K. (ed.). *Synopsis of the Four Gospels*. New York: American Bible Society; Stuttgart: German Bible Society, 1979. 3rd ed. The English translation of the previous entry, this volume offers the Greek text of the Nestle-Aland 26th edition (**10-007**) and the English of the RSV on facing pages. To make room for the English text, the rich apocryphal and patristic citations of the original are omitted. Probably the preferable edition for many without a technical interest; a "Quick Greek" resource. Structured on the two-source hypothesis.

14-002    Aland, K. (ed.). *Synopsis Quattuor Evangelorum*. New York: American Bible Society; Stuttgart: German Bible Society, 1978. 10th ed. One of two technical triumphs, this is a scholar's synopsis. Boasting a rich list of parallels from apocryphal gospels and patristic Christian sources, nothing comes close to providing so much relevant background material. The introduction is in both German and English.

14-003    Farmer, W. R. *Synopticon.* Cambridge University Press, 1969. Farmer's multi-colored method may sometimes be helpful in showing at a glance the extent of verbal agreement in a passage, but it is generally safer and more convenient to have synoptic texts printed side-by-side as in a traditional synopsis.

14-004    Francis, F. O. and J. P. Sampley (eds.). *Pauline Parallels.* Philadelphia: Fortress, n.d. Using the RSV text, the editors juxtapose closely related passages from the Pauline epistles and include relevant material from Acts.

14-005    Huck, A. *Synopsis of the First Three Gospels.* 9th ed., rev. by H. Keitzmann. Tübingen: Mohr/Siebeck, 1950; English edition by F. L. Cross; Oxford: Blackwell, 1957. An indispensable tool for the study of the Synoptic Gospels. Parallels from the Agrapha are added in footnotes; its *apparatus criticus* is restricted, but useful.

14-006    Huck, A. and H. Greeven (eds.). *Synopsis of the First Three Gospels with the Addition of the Johannine Parallels.* Grand Rapids: Eerdmans, 1981. 13th ed. Thoroughly revised since the 1936 edition, this edition has provided a newly edited text, making it completely independent of the Greek text common to both the UBS text (**10-001**) and the Nestle-Aland (**10-007**). All descriptive information is provided in both German and English. Technical and, for the scholar, indispensable. Structured on the two-source hypothesis.

14-007    Morgenthaler, R. *Statistische Synopse.* Zürich: Gotthelf-Verlag, 1971. A synopsis with a difference, this volume discusses the approaches of selected earlier synopses, setting out statistically the degree of verbal agreement and variations in the orders of the words, sentences and sections, and goes on to draw conclusions for the Synoptic Problem. A forbidding book, but full of valuable information for the specialist on the Synoptic Problem.

14-008    Orchard, Bernard. *A Synopsis of the Four Gospels in Greek Arranged according to the Two-Gospel Hypothesis.* Macon, GA: Mercer University Press, 1983. Edition is available in either English or Greek. The author lumps all other synopses together as "accepting the priority of Mark." This synopsis favors chronological sequence, i.e., Matthew, Luke, and Mark. Contains parallel columns reflecting this conclusion regarding the synoptic problem. Includes synoptics as well as John.

14-009    Sparks, H. F. D. *A Synopsis of the Gospels: The Synoptic Gospels with Johannine Parallels.* Philadelphia: Fortress Press, 1964.

14-010    Swanson, R. J. *The Horizontal Line Synopsis of the Gospels.* Western North Carolina Press, 1975. A "visual aid," this volume prints the parallels under one another, underlining areas of agreement. For the nonspecialist, this make precise word-for-word comparison far easier than in the conventional format of parallel columns.

14-011    Thomas, R. L. and S. N. Gundry (eds.). *A Harmony of the Gospels with Explanations and Essays.* Chicago: Moody Press, 1978. In addition to the standard harmony, the editors offer a useful index which allows the reader to locate any passage quickly. Also contains tables of cross-references, two maps, time-lines, and a set of essays, one of which defends the legitimacy of reading the gospel as a harmony, while another attacks the position of modern gospel scholarship. Conservative in perspective.

14-012    Throckmorton, B. H., Jr. (ed.). *Gospel Parallels: A Synopsis of the First Three Gospels.* 4th ed. Nashville: Nelson, 1979. With ample-sized pages and column widths designed not to frustrate the reader, this is the second-best synopsis available in English. This new edition expands the index of parallel passages not found in canonical NT literature. Brief introductory materials increase the usefulness of this book. Analytical, excellent, and compact, it offers many fewer parallels from John's gospel and from extracanonical literature.

# CHAPTER 15

# Software Programs

The explosion of the use of the PC in biblical studies is evidenced by the growth of the SBL-sponsored CARG (Computer Assisted Research Group), by the popularity of the ''Offline'' column published in both *The Bulletin of the Council of Societies for the Study of Religion* and in *Religious Studies News*, by the growing number of hypertext excursions available on the Internet, by the constant introduction of new software, and by the appearance of hundreds of projects dedicated to encoding and manipulating countless texts. These powerful tools and programs are bringing unbelievable speed, access, and convenience to the study of the Bible. Unfortunately, many scholars have not embraced the new technology in any meaningful way. This chapter attempts to review some of the specific software programs that are available, including search programs for the various texts, grammatical resources, multilingual word processors, Greek/Hebrew study aids, etc.

In the following pages the reference number is accompanied by a superscript character which indicates:

c=CD-ROM

d=DOS (IBM compatible)

m=Apple/Macintosh

w=MicroSoft Windows

15-001[c]     ABS Reference Bible on CD-ROM (American Bible Society, 1865 Broadway, New York NY 10023). KJV, NKJV, RSV, NRSV, NASV, TEV, German Bible (Luther), BHS Hebrew OT, UBS 3rd Greek, Rahlf's Septuagint, Latin Vulgate, English translation of the Septuagint, Hebrew Harmony of the Gospels, Greek Harmony of the Gospels, English Harmony of the Gospels, Apostolic Fathers in English, Works of Josephus, Dictionary of Bible and Religion. A complete reference library of Bible versions and resources.

15-002[c]     ATLA Religion Database: Special Series–Biblical Studies (American Theological Library Association, 820 Church Street, Evanston IL 60201). This resource consisting of approximately 90,000 references to periodicals articles and articles in multi-author collections (published 1949-1993) has just been released in mid-1994.

15-003[d]     Bible Link (Eagle Computing, P.O. Box 490, Elizabethton TN 37644). KJV, Greek and Hebrew lexicons. Offers hypertext-based text management, multiple windows, and a built-in word processor. Links specific words to their lexicon definition, or from a single occurrence to all the verses that contain the term. Searches both the English and Greek/Hebrew words.

**15-004<sup>dm</sup>** Bible Master (American Bible Sales, 870 S. Anaheim Boulevard, Anaheim CA 92805). KJV, NASB, Hebrew/Greek Dictionaries. TSR program permits the user to import text into any standard word processor for editing and printing. Offers powerful search features, and displays parallel verses.

**15-005<sup>d</sup>** Bible Source (Zondervan Electronic Publishing. 5300 Patterson Avenue SE, Grand Rapids MI 49530). NIV, KJV, NASB, NIV Exhaustive Concordance, NIV Study Bible Notes, NIV Bible Dictionary, An Encyclopedia of Bible Difficulties, Greek NT, Analytical NIV Concordance. May be purchased in individual modules, including Bible translations, original language texts, and related resources that work either separately or in tandem. Features pull-down menus with multiple onscreen Windows. Offers parallel display of text. Has built-in word processor.

**15-006<sup>w</sup>** Bible Windows (Silver Mountain Software, 1029 Tanglewood, Cedar Hill TX 75014). KJV, RSV with Apocrypha, tagged Greek Testament, tagged Hebrew OT (BHS), Septuagint, Latin Vulgate, Greek Dictionary, Hebrew Dictionary. Interlinear display, onscreen description of all grammatical tags, synchronized windows, dictionary search of Greek and Hebrew words. Fonts include Greek, Hebrew, Coptic, and Latin. Allows grammatical searching in Greek and Hebrew. Offers the Greek NT and Septuagint with complete locations of all words together with a comprehensive Greek Dictionary. Permits interlinear display of Greek and English.

**15-007<sup>d</sup>** Bible Word Plus (Hermenutika Computer Bible Research Software, P.O. Box 98563 Seattle WA 98198). KJV (with Apocrypha), RSV (with Apocrypha), NIV, UBS 3rd/Nestle-Aland 26th Greek NT (**10-007**), Hebrew OT, and Rahlf's Septuaginta Greek OT. Full accented Greek onscreen. Permits exporting Greek and Hebrew text into a multilingual word processor such as Multilingual Scholar (**15-017**) and ChiWriter (**15-010**).

**15-008<sup>w</sup>** Bibleworks for Windows (Hermenutika Computer Bible Research Software, P.O. Box 98563, Seattle WA 98198). KJV, RSV (with Apocrypha), ASV (1901), UBS 3rd/Nestle-Aland 26th Greek NT (**10-007**), Hebrew OT, Rahlf's Septuagint Greek OT, and Latin Vulgate, Strong's Concordance,

Englishman's Concordance, 100,000 Greek and Hebrew words with locations, Thayer's Greek Lexicon, Brown-Driver Briggs Hebrew Lexicon, The Treasury of Scripture Knowledge. For the advanced student, this comprehensive program provides many features not found in other software, e.g., extensive list of translations and resources, Greek/Hebrew texts. Offers grammatical searches of the Greek and Hebrew texts. Words may be analyzed grammatically analyzed with full location and lexical root. The Multi Document Interface (MDI) editor, which supports Greek, Hebrew (including automatic right-to-left layouts), allows the texts to be imported into any standard Windows-based word processor.

15-009$^c$   CD Word Library (Logos Research Systems, 200th Avenue West, Oak Harbor WA 98277). KJV, NIV, NASV, RSV, Greek NT, Septuagint, Bauer-Arndt-Gingrich (BAG), Liddell and Scott lexicon, Theological Dictionary of the NT, New Bible Dictionary, Harper's Bible Dictionary, Harper's Bible Commentary, Bible Knowledge Commentary, Jerome Bible Commentary. Emphasizes Greek study references. Usual searches and interactions facilities for both the texts and resources.

15-010$^d$   Chiwriter (Horstmann Software, P.O. Box 1807, San Jose CA 95109). With multilingual capabilities, Chiwriter offers traditional word processing in multiple fonts and languages, including Greek and Hebrew. The program is WYSIWYG and includes a font designer. It support a variety of printers.

15-011$^d$   Everyword Good News Bible (American Bible Society, 1865 Broadway, New York NY 10023). TEV. Offers usual textual manipulations including the ability to save text and materials to a clipboard for further operations or integration with other documents. Includes WordPerfect Jr. providing fully-featured word processing.

15-012$^d$   Gramcord (Gramcord Institute, 2218 NE Brookview Drive, Vancouver WA 98686). Offers an integrated concordance system for examining the word of the OT and the NT. Is capable of conducting advanced searches relating to syntax. The Gramcord Institute publishes other study tools such as Gramsearch, GramGreek, and Parser Plus.

15-013$^d$   Greek Tools (Parsons Technology, P.O. Box 100, Hiawatha IA 52233-0100). This Greek lexicon database with grammar guide includes manuscript evidence, and thus permits the user to function as a text critic. The program also includes a multilingual word processor.

**15-014<sup>dw</sup>** Holy Scriptures (Christian Technologies, P.O. Box 2201, Independence MO 64055). KJV, ASV, RSV (with Apocrypha), NRSV (with Apocrypha), NIV, New American Bible with Revised NT (Catholic), The Living Bible, Greek and Hebrew transliteration and definitions. Offers a wide range of translations and includes the basic search and display features.

**15-015<sup>dm</sup>** LBASE (Silver Mountain Software, 1029 Tanglewood, Cedar Hill TX 75014). Permits grammatical studies of various texts, including the Greek, Hebrew, LXX, as well as Latin texts. Includes a concordance.

**15-016<sup>w</sup>** Logos Bible Software (Logos Research Systems, 2117 200th Avenue West, Oak Harbor WA 98277). KJV, NKJV, NIV, RSV, NRSV, ASV 1901, Byzantine/Majority Textform, Nestle-Aland 26th/UBS 3rd, Textus Receptus, Hebrew text, The Treasury of Scripture Knowledge, Strong's Lexicon, TVM (Tense Voice Mood), Nave's Topical Bible. Offers a strong, graphical, visual approach to textual studies. Includes numerous pull-down menus, button bars, and multiple windows. Ideal for the advanced student. Permits efficient searches using English, Greek, and Hebrew. Allows for onscreen fonts.

**15-017<sup>d</sup>** Multilingual Scholar (Gamma Productions, 710 Wilshire Boulevard, Suite 609, Santa Monica CA 90401). Supports a wide range of languages, including Greek and Hebrew, and includes word processing features.

**15-018<sup>c</sup>** The New Bible Library (Ellis Enterprises, 4205 McAuley Blvd., Suite 385, Oklahoma City OK 73120). ASV, Chronological Bible (KJV), KJV, Literal English Translation with Strong's Numbers, The Living Bible, MicroBible, New American Bible with Revised NT, NASB, NIV, New Jerusalem Version, NKIV, RSV, Simple English Bible (NT), Transliterated Bible, and Transliterated Pronounceable Bible, Harris's Theological Wordbook of the OT, Strong's Greek and Hebrew Dictionary, Vine's Expository Dictionary of Old and NT Words, Barclay's Daily Bible Study Series, Gray's Bible Study Notes, Matthew Henry's Concise Commentary of the Whole Bible, Morris's

114

Introduction to the Books of the Bible, the Complete Works of Josephus, Easton's Bible Dictionary, Edersheim's Life and Times of Jesus, Elwell's Evangelical Dictionary of Theology, and 12 Bible Maps. This comprehensive resource package features a wide selection of translations as well a variety of resources. Employs IBM's SoftCopy Navigator system to enable easy management of the enormous amount of information.

**15-019**dc    Online Bible (P.O. Box 21, Branson MI 49028). KJV, NIV, RSV, Greek and Hebrew texts, The Treasury of Scripture Knowledge, King James lexicon. This is a low-cost, full-featured, yet comprehensive program. Its features the standard searching and displaying. Includes a built-in text editor.

**15-020**dw    PC Study Bible (Biblesoft, 22014 Seventh Avenue S. #201, Seattle WA 98198). KJV, NIV, ASV, RSV, NKIV, and The Living Bible, Exhaustive Concordance, Nave's Topical Bible, Nelson's Bible Dictionary, Strong's Dictionary, Englishman's Concordance, Vine's Expository Dictionary of Biblical Words, and The Treasury of Scripture Knowledge. Available in three separate modules (these may be purchased separately and used together). All editions feature a concordance and an integrated word processor. Allows for multiple, overlapping windows on the screen permitting the user to view several translations and resources simultaneously.

**15-021**dw    Quick Verse (Parsons Technology, P.O. Box 100, Hiawatha IA 52233). KJV, NKJV, NIV, RSV, NRSV, The Living Bible, Hebrew and Greek Transliterated Bibles, Nave's Topical Bible. The DOS version is a multi-featured Bible system that provides a full range of texts. The windows version offers multiple onscreen windows. Both offer the usual search features for words, phrases, etc.

**15-022**d    Scripture Fonts (Zondervan Electronic Publishing, 5300 Patterson Avenue SE, Grand Rapids MI 49530). This TSR program enables the users of Word Perfect 5.0 or 5.1 to have onscreen Greek and Hebrew characters (with complete accenting and pointing), and to print these within documents on a wide range of printers.

**15-023**w    Universe for Windows (Gamma Productions, 710 Wilshire Boulevard, Suite 609, Santa Monica CA 90401). Features a wide range of languages and fonts. Permits foreign spell checking and alternate keyboard layouts. Allows easy WYSIWYG creation of foreign words and dozens of supported languages. With LanguageLink it possible to use some of the supported languages within other Windows applications.

15-024$^d$    The Word: Advanced Study System (Words of Word Inc., 5221 North O'Connor Blvd., Suite 1000, Irving TX 75039). KJV, NKJV, NRSV, Hebrew OT, Greek NT, Strong's Concordance/Dictionary. Provides a graphical user interface without the necessity of Windows. Offers advanced tools for Greek and Hebrew. Features an easy-to-use graphical interface that is ideal for both beginners and advanced users. Allows multiple onscreen windows (these may be moved, resized, and iconified) which can be linked together to display the same verse in various translations or languages or resources.

15-025$^{dw}$    The Word Processor (Bible Research Systems, 2013 Wells Branch Parkway #304, Austin TX 78728). KJV, NKJV, NIV, RSV, and Strong's Concordance. Librarian, Personal Commentary, Chain Reference, Topics, People, Chronological Bible, Verse Typist. Provides access to various texts. Includes the standard search and retrieval features. Supports multiple synchronized windows for viewing multiple translations. Also offers add-on packages that are designed for the more specialized and advanced students, such as support for topical and chronological studies and studies of geography and biblical terms.

15-026$^d$    Wordsearch (Navpress Software, P.O. Box 3500, Colorado Springs CO 80935). KJV, NKJV, NIV, NRSV, New American Bible, The Living Bible, Strong's Ties to the Greek and Hebrew, and Nave's Topics. Offers great flexibility in defining searches in very specific and detailed ways. Features include split screens for viewing multiple translations, pull-down menus, and fast searches (usually one-two seconds).

# CHAPTER 16

# Libraries: Their Nature and Use

The extant literature for the study of the NT is so voluminous, serious study hardly occurs apart from the utilization of a major library. This chapter aims to provide an orientation to library use by providing a discussion of certain introductory materials that relate to general library usage.

## Classification Systems

The "classification" of books differs from the "cataloguing" of books even though the two functions are closely related. Cataloguing is the technical process whereby the library staff produces a record for the book. This record (historically a card in the card catalogue, though in recent years some libraries utilize microfiche cards or an on-line computer terminal) becomes a permanent part of the library's system for directing the reader to a specific location in the collection. Cataloguing thus entails describing the book in terms of the author and title, and by providing other relevant publication data that often includes certain physical characteristics of the book. Finally, cataloguing procedures require that a subject access descriptor be assigned to the book. This descriptor will determine where the resultant card appears in the cataloguing system.

Classification is obviously related to the cataloguing process, but is a distinct operation. Simply, classification refers to the process whereby the various materials are organized according to subject and then given a call number that makes retrieval possible.

There are two classification systems[1] in use at the major theological libraries in the United States: Dewey Decimal Classification System and the Library of Congress Classification System (LC). Many libraries use both systems, assigning more recent books within the Library of Congress Classification System. Some are gradually converting the older collection from Dewey to LC.

**Dewey Decimal System**

In use for more than 100 years, this system was originally developed by Melvil Dewey. It has undergone constant revision[2] so that it will reflect the changing and ever-broadening areas of knowledge.

---

[1] A third system, known as the Pettee System, is in use at the Library of the Union Theological Seminary in Richmond, Virginia. The system is somewhat similar to the LC system and is named for its originator, Julia Pettee. See Julia Pettee, "A Classification for a Theological Library," *Library Journal* 36 (1911): 611-24.

[2] The revisions are published by the Lake Placid Foundation, Forest Press, Inc., Lake Placid, NY 12948.

The Dewey has ten major categories. Each is divided into numerous sub-categories. These sub-categories are further divided into sub-sets that are virtually unlimited. These "sub" divisions are made decimally, hence the name.

According to Dewey, the ten divisions of knowledge are as follows:

General Works; Philosophy; Religion; Social Sciences, Sociology; Philology; Pure Science; Useful Arts; Fine Arts, Recreation; Literature; History.

Within the major division of religion are the following subdivisions: Religion; Philosophy & Theories of Religion; Handbooks & Outlines; Dictionaries & Encyclopedias; Essays & Lectures; Periodicals; Organizations & Societies; Study & Teaching; Collections; History; Natural Theology; Knowledge of God; Pantheism; Creation; Theodicy; Religion & Science; Good & Evil; Worship; Immortality; Analogy; Bible; OT; Historical Books; Poetic Books; Prophetic Books; NT; Gospels & Acts; Epistles; Revelation; Apocrypha; Doctrinal Theology; God; Christology; Man; Salvation; Angels, Devils, Satan; Eschatology; Future State; Christian Creeds; Apologetics; Devotional & Practical; Moral Theology; Meditations; Evangelistic Writings; Miscellany; Hymnology; Christian Symbolism; Sacred Furniture & Vestments; Personal Religions; Family Worship; Pastoral Theology; Preaching (Homiletics); Sermons; Pastor; Church Administration; Brotherhoods & Sisterhoods; Societies; Education Work; Parish Welfare Work; Other Parish Work; Christian Church; Christian Social Theology; Government & Organization; Sabbath, Lord's Day, & sunday; Public Worship, Ritual, & Liturgy; Sacraments & Ordinances; Missions; Religious Associations; Religious Education and Sunday Schools; Revivals & Spiritual Renewal; Christian Church History; Religious Orders; Persecutions; Heresies; In Europe; In Asia; In Africa; In North America; In South America; Other Parts of the World; Christian Churches & Sects; Primitive & Oriental Churches; Roman Catholic Church; Anglican Churches; Protestantism; Presbyterian & Congregational Churches; Baptist &

Immersionist Churches; Methodist Churches; Unitarian Churches; Other christian Sects; Other Religions; Comparative Religion; Greek & Roman; Teutonic & Norse Religions; Brahmanism & Buddhism; Zoroastrianism & Related; Judaism; Islam & Bahaism; Open Classification; Other Non-Christian Religions.

Of particular concern in this handbook is the classification "220." Therein is one of the major weaknesses of the Dewey System. In a large theological library there will be so many sub-sub and sub-sub-sub categories crowded into the 220's that the number of decimal places necessary becomes cumbersome. In smaller libraries the system offers great simplicity since the Arabic system is easily understood. Also, many trade bibliographies are keyed to the Dewey System.

**Library of Congress Classification**

This system was developed for the Library of Congress and is a part of that library's card catalogue service. Today, libraries that are computer oriented often make use of the "MARC format" program in which computer tapes are offered to participating libraries. The cataloguing scheme involves both numbers and letters, and, like Dewey, is constantly kept up to date.[3]

The basic (alpha) divisions to which the subdivisions (numeric) apply are as follows:

A    General Works, Polygraphy

B    Philosophy, Religion

C    History, Auxiliary Sciences

---

[3]Updates are available from the Card Division, Library of Congress, Building 159, Navy Yard Annex, Washington, DC 20541.

D       History and Topography (except America)

E-F     America

G       Geography, Anthropology, Sports

H       Social Sciences

J       Political Science

K       Law

L       Education

M       Music

N       Fine Arts

P       Language and Literature

PN      Literary History and Literature

Q       Science

R       Medicine

S       Agriculture, Plant and Animal Industry

T       Technology

U       Military Science

V       Science

Z       Bibliography

Within the general category "B", there follows the breakdown of the "BS" subdivision:

1937-1965    The Greek NT

1937         Collections

1937.5       Comparative texts of Greek NT

1938         History and criticism

                  Manuscripts. Codices

1939         General works

Individual manuscripts in facsimile

| | |
|---|---|
| 1964 | By name, A-Z |
| 1964.5 | By number |
| 1965 | Modern printed editions. By date |
| 1966 | Selections from the Greek NT |
| 1967-1990 | Latin versions |
| 1990 | Modern Latin versions |
| 1992-1994 | Syriac versions |
| 1992 | Texts. By date |

Manuscripts. Codices

| | |
|---|---|
| 1992.3 | General works |
| 1992.5 | Individual manuscripts in facsimile, A-Z |
| 1993 | Special versions. By name, A-Z |
| .2 | Texts. By date |
| .3-5 | Manuscripts. Codices |
| 1994 | History and criticism |
| 1995-2020 | Other early versions |
| 1995-1996 | Armenian |
| 2000-2001 | Coptic |
| 2005-2006 | Ethiopic |
| 2010-2011 | Hebrew |
| 2015-2016 | Church Slavic |
| 2020 | Other, A-Z |
| 2025-2213 | Modern texts and versions of the NT |
| 2025-2098 | English |
| 2070-2071 | Geneva, 1557 |
| 2080-2081 | Rheims, 1582 |

| | |
|---|---|
| 2099-2213 | Other modern European languages |
| 2261 | English |
| 2262 | Dutch |
| 2263 | French |
| 2264 | German |
| 2265 | Italian |
| 2266 | Scandinavian |
| 2267 | Spanish and Portuguese |
| 2269 | Other languages, A-Z |
| 2301-2312 | Concordances |
| 2301 | Hebrew |
| 2302 | Greek |
| 2303 | Latin |
| 2305 | English |
| 2306 | French |
| 2307 | German |
| 2308 | Other languages, A-Z |
| 2310 | Topical indices, references, tables, etc |
| 2312 | Dictionaries |
| 2315-2325 | Introductory works. History of the NT |
| 2315 | General works |
| 2316 | History of translations of the NT |
| 2317 | The English NT |
| 2318 | The NT in other modern European languages, A-Z |
| 2320 | Canon |
| 2325 | Textual criticism |
| 2329-2332 | General works. Introductions |

| | |
|---|---|
| 2329 | Early to 1800 |
| 2330 | 1801-1950 |
| 2330.2 | 1951- |
| 2331 | Hermeneutics. Exegetics. Principles of interpretation |
| 2332 | Inspiration. Authenticity |
| 2333-2348 | Commentaries |
| 2333 | Early to 1950 |
| .2 | 1951- |
| .5 | Sermons. Meditations, Devotions |
| 2335-2335.5 | Latin |
| 2340 | Early to 1800 |
| 2341 | 1801-1950 |
| .2 | 1951- |
| 2342 | Dutch |
| 2343 | French |
| 2344 | German |
| 2345 | Italian |
| 2346 | Scandinavian |
| 2347 | Spanish and Portuguese |
| 2348 | Other languages, A-Z |
| 2350-2395 | Criticism and interpretation |
| 2350 | History of NT criticism and interpretation |
| 2351 | Biography, A-Z |
| 2353 | Greek |
| 2355 | Latin |
| 2360-2368 | Other languages, A-Z |
| 2370 | General special |

| 2372 | Rationalistic works |
|---|---|
| 2375 | Historical criticism |
| 2376 | Eschatological school of criticism |
| 2377 | Form criticism |
| 2378 | Demythologization |
| 2385 | Word studies (General and individual) |
| 2387 | Relations of the OT and NT |
| 2390 | Other works |
| 2391 | Mythological, allegorical, numerical, astronomical interpretations of the NT |
| 2393 | Addresses, essays, etc., on NT criticism |
| 2395 | Addresses, essays, etc., on the NT in general |
| 2397 | Theology of the NT |
| 2407-2410 | NT history |
| 2408 | Study and teaching |
| 2409 | NT chronology |
| 2410 | History of Christianity in NT times |
| 2415 | The teachings of Jesus |
| 2415.A2 | Selections from Scripture |
| 2415.A3 | Other collections |
| 2415.A4-Z | General works. The belief of Jesus |
| 2430-2520 | Biography |
| 2430 | General works |
| 2431 | Sermons |
| 2440 | Lives of the Apostles and disciples |
| 2441 | Lives of the evangelists |
| 2445 | Women in the NT |
| 2446 | Children in the NT |

| | |
|---|---|
| 2448 | Other special, A-Z |
| 2450 | A-Andrew |
| 2451 | Andrew, Saint, apostle |
| 2452 | Andrew-James |
| 2453 | James, Saint, apostle |
| 2454 | James-John |
| 2455 | John, Saint, apostle |
| 2456 | John the Baptist |
| 2458 | Joseph, Saint |
| 2460 | Joseph-Luke |
| 2465 | Luke, Saint |
| 2470 | Luke-Mark |
| 2475 | Mar, Saint |
| 2480 | Mark-Mary |
| 2485 | Mary Magdalene, Saint |
| 2490 | Mary-Matthew |
| 2495 | Matthew, Saint, apostle |
| 2500 | Matthew-Paul |
| 2505.A3 | Paul, Saint, apostle |
| 2510 | Paul-Peter |
| 2515 | Peter, Saint, apostle |
| 2520 | Peter-Z |
| 2525 | Study and teaching |
| 2525 | Outlines, syllabi, etc |
| 2530 | General works |
| 2534-35 | English textbooks |
| 2536 | Catholic textbooks |

| | |
|---|---|
| 2537 | French textbooks |
| 2538 | German textbooks |
| 2539 | Italian textbooks |
| 2540 | Scandinavian textbooks |
| 2541 | Spanish and Portuguese textbooks |
| 2542 | Other languages, A-Z. Textbooks |
| 2543 | Minor works |
| 2545 | Topics (not otherwise provided for) A-Z |
| 2547-2559 | Special parts of the NT |
| 2547 | Epistles and gospels, Liturgical |
| 2548 | Gospels and Acts of the Apostles |
| 2549 | Polyglot texts |
| 2550 | West Syriac |
| 2550.5 | East Syriac |
| 2551 | Greek |
| 2552 | Latin |
| 2553 | English |
| 2554 | Other European languages, A-Z |
| 2555 | Criticism. Commentaries, etc |
| 2556 | Study and teaching |
| 2557 | Paraphrases, English |
| 2559 | Chronology of the Gospels |
| 2560 | Harmonies of the Gospels |
| 2570-2575.5 | Matthew |
| 2580-2585.5 | Mark |
| 2590-2595.5 | Luke |
| 2610-2615.5 | John |

2620-2625.5   Acts of the Apostles

2630-2635.5   Epistles

2660-2665.5   Romans

2670-2675.5   Corinthians, I and II

2680-2685.5   Galatians

2690-2695.5   Ephesians

2700-2705.5   Philippians

2710-2715.5   Colossians

2720-2725.5   Thessalonians, I and II

2730-2735.5   Pastoral epistles

2740-2745.5   Timothy, I and II

2750-2755.5   Titus

2760-2765.5   Philemon

2770-2775.5   Hebrews

2777          General epistles. Catholic epistles

2780-2785.5   James

2790-2795.5   Peter, I and II

2800-2805.5   John, I, II, and III

2810-2815.5   Jude

2820-2825.5   Apocalypse. Revelations

2827          Apocalypse and history

2831-2970     NT Apocrypha

2840          History and criticism

2851          History and criticism

2860          Individuals Gospels, A-Z

2870-2871     Acts

2890-2891     Epistles

2910-2911    Apocalypses

2930-2931    Didactic works

2950-2951    Doctrinal works

2970         Apocryphal writings and sayings of Jesus

# Research and Writing

16-001    Aldrich, Ella Virginia and Thomas Edward Camp. *Using Theological Books and Libraries*. Prentice-Hall, 1963. This guide lists approximately 500 reference tools in theology and generally introduces their use. Includes information on bibliographies, dictionaries, indices, abstracts, and encyclopedias, etc. There are title and subject indices.

16-002    Anderson, Margaret J. *The Christian Writer's Handbook*. Harper and Row, 1974. This volume deals with matters of style, form, information on short stories, etc. A brief bibliography and an index are provided.

16-003    Barzun, Jacques and Henry Franklin Graff. *The Modern Researcher*. 3rd ed. Harcourt Brace Jovanovich, 1977. The volume covers principles, research methodology and writing techniques, etc. Designed primarily for beginners.

16-004    Bolich, Gregory G. *The Christian Scholar: An Introduction to Theological Research*. University Press of America, 1986. This introductory volume reviews research methodologies and data analysis techniques often used in theological research. The 337 page volume is divided into three parts, each following logically the other: (1) an introduction to research; (2) an introduction to methods and models of theological research; (3) examples of these principals of research applied to specific study areas.

16-005    Bollier, John A. *The Literature of Theology: A Guide for Students and Pastors*. Westminster Press, 1979. A good, general introduction for the beginning student. Covers "the Bible" as well as "parts" of the Bible, but also systematic theology, church history and denominational studies.

16-006    Campbell, William Giles. *Form and Style in Thesis Writing*. Houghton Mifflin Company, 1954. A good bit simpler than the *Manual of Style* (**16-028**), this guide has been used for years in the preparation of theses and dissertations. Actual sample pages show the difference between footnotes and bibliographic citations for the same titles.

16-007     Chaplin, A. H. (comp.). *Names of Persons: National Usages for Entry in Catalogues.* IFLA/FIAB, 1967. Describes how to catalogue names from more than 60 countries of the world.

16-008     Dawe, Grosvenor. *Melvil Dewey: Seer, Inspirer, Doer.* Lake Placid Club, 1932. This volume documents the life and contributions of Melvil Dewey.

16-009     Gorman, Michael and Paul W. Winkler. *Anglo-American Cataloguing Rules.* 2nd ed. Chicago: American Library Association, 1978. This volume is not for the general reader but may be helpful in seeking specific information in a specific research area before beginning intensive research. Helps to enable the student to understand how materials may have been entered into the cataloguing system.

16-010     Hutchins, Margaret. *Introduction to Reference Work.* Chicago: American Library Association, 1944. A very helpful general introduction. Relates to all fields, but provides some general overview of the nature and purpose of reference works in "any field."

16-011     Kennedy, James R., Jr. *Library Research Guide to Religion and Theology: Illustrated Search Strategy and Sources.* Library Research Guides Series 1. Pierian Press, 1974. An excellent study guide for the beginner, this very basic manual covers the choice of research topic, card catalogues, evaluation of books, data collecting, and using guides to religious publications.

16-012     Kepple, Robert J. *Reference Works for Theological Research.* University Press of America, 1981.

16-013     Lenroot-Ernt, Lois (ed.). *Subject Directory of Special Libraries and Information Centers.* 5 vols. Gale Research Co., 1982. The information of interest to researchers in the field of NT studies may be found in volume 4, pages 323-89, "Theological Libraries 3374-4275."

16-014     Leunen, Mary-Claire van. *A Handbook for Scholars.* Alfred A. Knopf, 1978. A handbook for dealing with problems unique to scholarly writing: citations, quotations, footnotes, references, bibliographies, and manuscript preparation.

Contains index. Questions of style can be answered by consulting the *Chicago Manual of Style* (**16-028**).

**16-015**    Lubans, John, Jr. *Educating the Library User*. Bowker, 1974. An anthology that covers libraries of various kinds. Includes a discussion on computer assisted instruction.

**16-016**    Montgomery, John Warwick. *The Writing of Research Papers in Theology: An Introductory Lecture with A List of Basic Reference Tools for the Theological Student*. Trinity Evangelical Divinity School, 1959. An introductory lecture for the beginner, this guide places research and writing within the wider context of theological study. Contains a list of 150 reference tools.

**16-017**    O'Rourke, William Thomas. *Library Handbook for Catholic Readers*. Bruce Publishing Company, 1937. This is a general guide to libraries and literature for the general reader but contains advanced appendices useful to Catholic students of theology.

**16-018**    Punt, Neal R. *Baker's Textual and Topical Filing System*. Baker Book House, 1960. A guide outlining a simple system for organizing study materials and using a minimal amount of time and effort.

**16-019**    Quirk, Randolph, et al. *A Grammar of Contemporary English*. Longman Group, 1972. This detailed reference grammar of English incorporates recent research into present day English syntax. Contains appendices, bibliography, and index.

**16-020** .    Sayre, John L. *A Manual of Forms for Research Papers and D.Min. Field Project Reports*. Seminary Press, 1981. A step-by-step handbook specifically designed for use by students of theology in the preparation of a research paper or report. Contains examples of title pages, tables of contents, footnotes, bibliographies, and other appendices. See also *Manual of Forms for Term Papers and Theses* (**16-021**).

**16-021**    Sayre, John L. *A Manual of Forms for Term Papers and Theses*. 4th ed. Seminary Press, 1973. Designed to guide students in the preparation of term papers, field projects, and theses, this basic manual of forms includes samples of appendices and indices. For more detailed guides, see *Chicago Manual* *of Style* (**16-028**), Sayre's *Manual of Forms for Research Papers and D.Min. Field Project Reports* (**16-020**), Turabian's *Manual for Writers of Term Papers, Theses, and Dissertations* (**16-027**), and Campbell's *Form and Style in Thesis Writing* (**16-006**).

**16-022**  Sayre, John L. and Roberta Hamburger (comp.). *An Illustrated Guide to the Anglo-American Cataloguing Rules.* Enid, OK: Seminary Press, 1971. A how-to book that illustrates the *Anglo-American Cataloging Rules* with specific reference to theological libraries.

**16-023**  Shera, Jesse H. *Libraries and the Organization of Knowledge.* Archon Books, 1965. A good, general introduction for library orientation and use.

**16-024**  Sheehy, Eugene P. *Guide to Reference Books.* 9th ed. American Library Association, 1976. Arranged by subject and function, this is a basic working tool of reference librarians. Contains index.

**16-025**  Sheehy, Eugene P. *Guide to Reference Books, Supplement.* American Library Association, 1980. Supplement to Sheehy's original guide (**16-024**), this volume includes a large number of additional works published from mid-1973 to late 1978. Contains a section discussing computer-readable data bases.

**16-026**  Strunk, William. *The Elements of Style.* 2nd ed. McMillan Company, 1972. A brief volume concentrating on fundamental rules of English usage and principles of composition. For more detailed information, see Quirk's *A Grammar of Contemporary English* (**16-019**).

**16-027**  Turabian, Kate L. *A Manual for Writers of Term Papers, Theses, and Dissertations.* 4th ed. University of Chicago Press, 1973. A comprehensive guide for solving writing problems faced by students of all levels. For more detailed explanations, see *Chicago Manual of Style* (**16-028**).

**16-028**  University of Chicago Press. *Chicago Manual of Style for Authors, Editors, and Copywriters.* 13th ed., rev. and expanded. University of Chicago Press, 1982. The most comprehensive and useful guide for all writers. Covers material on style, grammar, bibliographies, and indices. Contains full subject index, detailed outlines of contents, glossary of technical terms, and a bibliography.

16-029    Waardenburg, Jean Jacques. *Classical Approaches to the Study of Religion. Aims, Methods, and Theories of Research.* Vol. 1- . Religion and Reason, vol. 3. Mouton, 1973- . A valuable source book for students of religion concerned with methodology, volume 1 is an introduction and anthology containing lengthy excerpts from writings of 40 scholars.

16-030    *World Guide to Libraries.* 4th ed. Part I: Verlag Documentation, 974. Vol. 8 of *Handbook of International Documentation and Information.*

# Index

## authors, editors, compilers

Abbott-Smith, G., 12-001

Ackroyd, Peter R., 2-025, 8-010

Adeney, Walter F., 8-011

Ahroni, Jochanan, 9-001

Aland, B., 10-001

Aland, Kurt, 2-026, 10-001, 13-001, 14-001, 14-002

Albright, William F., 8-012, 9-002, 9-003

Aldrich, Ella V., 16-001

Alford, Henry, 8-038

Allen, Clifton J., 8-013

Althaus, Paul, 8-055, 8-056

Anderson, George W., 2-028

Anderson, Margaret J., 16-002

Appel, H., 8-055

Armstrong, James F., 2-029

Aune, David E., 2-049

Avigad, N., 9-004

Bachmann, H., 13-002

Baer, Eleanora A., 2-015

Bailly, A., 12-002

Baly, Dennis, 9-005, 9-006, 9-007

Barclay, William, 8-014

Barrow, John G., 2-006

Barzun, Jacques, 16-003

Bauer, W., 12-003

Bauernfeind, O., 8-055

Behm, Johannes, 8-056

Berlin, Charles, 4-001

Berry, G. R., 12-004

Bestermann, Theodore, 2-001

Bilboul, Roger R., 6-002

Billerbeck, Paul, 8-061

Black, Dorothy M., 6-003

Black, J. Sutherland, 7-006

Black, Matthew, 8-001, 8-021

Blass, F., 11-001

Bolich, Gregory G., 16-004

Bollier, John A., 16-005

Bonet-Maury, G., 6-004

Bonnard, Pierre, 8-039

Bover, J. M., 10-002, 10-003

Bowdle, Donald N., 8-015

Bowman, John W., 2-050

Box, George H., 8-036

Briggs, Charles A., 8-023

Brock, Sebastien P., 2-032

Bromiley, G. W., 7-002, 7-003, 7-013

Brown, Colin, 7-004

Brown, Raymond E., 8-002

Bruce, F. F., 8-040

Buchard, Christoph, 2-033

Burton, E. DeW., 11-002

Buss, Martin J., 6-005

Buttrick, George A., 7-005, 8-016


Calvin, Jean., 8-017, 8-018

Camp, Thomas E., 16-001

Campbell, William G., 16-006

Carter, Charles W., 8-019

Chadwick, Henry, 8-042

Chamberlain, W. D., 11-003

Chantraine, P., 12-005

Chaplin, A. H., 16-007

Charlesworth, James H., 2-034

Cheyne, Thomas K., 7-006

Clarke, Adam, 8-020

Clarke, W. K. L., 8-003, 8-004

Clements, Ronald E., 8-021

Collison, Robert L., 2-003

Cremer, H., 12-006

Crim, K., 7-005

Cruden, A., 13-003


Dana, H. E., 11-004

Danker, F. W., 2-035, 12-003

Daris, S., 12-007

Darlow, T. H., 2-036

Darton, Michael, 13-004

David, W. H., 11-005, 11-014

Davidson, Francis, 8-022

Davis, J. D., 7-007

Dawe, Grosvenor, 16-008

De Marco, Angelus A., 2-051

Debrunner A., 11-001

Delling, Gerhard, 2-037

Dever, W. G., 9-008

Doty, William G., 2-052

Douglas, J. D., 7-008

Driver, Samuel R., 8-023

Duplacy, J., 2-053

Dykers, P., 2-034


Earle, Ralph, 8-019

Edwards, R. A., 13-005

Eiselen, Frederick C., 8-005

Ellicott, Charles J., 8-025

Ellison, John W., 13-006

Erbacher, Hermann, 2-040

Erdman, Charles R., 8-026


Farmer, W. R., 14-003

Fascher, Erich, 8-058

Filson, Floyd V., 9-020

Finegan, Jack, 9-009

Fitzmyer, Joseph A., 2-042, 2-043, 8-002

France, R. T., 2-054

Francis, F. O., 14-004

Freedman, David N., 8-012

Frisk, H., 12-008

Fritsch, Charles J., 2-032

Fuller, R., 8-006


Gaebelein, Frank E., 8-027

Gaffron, H.-G., 2-055

Gall, J., 13-007

Gaston, L., 13-008

Geden, A. S., 13-016

Gehman, Henry S., 7-010

Gignac, F. T., 11-006

Gingrich, F. W., 12-003, 12-009

Glanzman, George S., 2-043

Gorman, Michael, 16-009

Gottcent, John H., 2-044

Graff, Henry F., 16-003

Grant, Frederick C., 8-028

Gray, Richard A., 2-004

Greeven, H., 14-006

Grollenberg, Lucas H., 9-010

Gundry, S. N., 14-011

Hadidian, D. Y., 2-056

Hamburger, Roberta, 2-021, 4-017, 16-022

Hartdegen, S. J., 13-009

Hastings, James, 7-011

Hatch, E., 13-010

Hawkins, John., 13-011

Hendriksen, William, 8-043

Herbert, Arthur S., 2-045

Hester, Goldia, 2-046

Hester, James, 2-047, 2-048

Hillyer, N., 7-012

Hines, Theodore C., 4-009

Hort, F. J. A., 10-010

Howard, F. W., 11-012

Howley, G. C. D., 8-044

Hubbard, D. A., 8-029

Huck, A., 14-005, 14-006

Humphreys, H. M., 2-057

Hurd, John C., 2-007

Hutchins, Margaret, 16-010


Jacques, X., 13-012

Jellicoe, Sidney, 2-032

Joy, Charles R., 13-013

Karavidopoulos, J., 10-001

Kareling, E. G. H., 9-011

Kelly, Balmer H., 8-030

Kelly, Genevieve, 2-047, 2-048

Kennedy, James R., 16-011

Kenyon, K., 9-012

Kepple, Robert J., 16-012

Kilpatrick, G. D., 10-004

Kissinger, Warren S., 2-058, 2-059

Kittel, G., 7-013

Koester, Helmut, 8-031

Kuss, Otto, 8-063

Lampe, G. W. H., 12-010

Lance, H. D., 9-008

Langevin, P.-E., 2-060

LaSor, W. S., 11-007

Laymon, Charles M., 8-007

Leaney, A. R. C., 8-010

Legg, S. C. E., 10-005

Lemmons, R. G., 7-021

Lenroot-Ernt, Lois, 16-013

Lenski, R. C. H., 8-045

Leunen, Mary-Claire van, 16-014

Liddell, H. G., 12-011, 12-012, 12-013

Lietzmann, Hans, 8-059

Lock, Walther, 8-032

Lubans, John, 16-015

Lyons, William N., 2-061, 2-062, 2-063

Machen, J. G., 11-008

Malatesta, Edward, 2-064

Mantey, J. R., 11-004

Marsh, John, 8-033

Marrow, S. B., 2-065

Martini, C. M., 10-001

Massyngbaerde, J., 8-053

Mattill, A. J., 2-066

Mattill, M. B., 2-066

May, Herbert G., 9-013

Mays, J. L., 8-008

Mayser, E., 11-009

McKenzie, J. L., 7-014

Meecham, H. G., 11-011

Merk, A., 10-006

Metzger, B. M., 2-067, 2-068, 2-069, 2-070, 2-071, 8-046, 10-001

Meyer, H. A. W., 8-047, 8-060

Miller, J. Lane, 7-015, 7-016

Miller, J. Maxwell, 9-014

Miller, Madelein S., 7-015, 7-016

Milligan, G., 12-015

Mills, Watson E., 2-072, 2-073, 2-074, 5-004, 7-017, 8-009

Moffatt, James, 8-048

Monson, J., 9-015

Montgomery, John W., 16-016

Moorey, R., 9-016

Morgenthaler, R., 13-014, 14-007

Morrison, C., 13-015

Moule, C. F. D., 8-049, 11-010

Moule, H. F., 2-036

Moulton, H. K., 12-014

Moulton, J. H., 11-011, 11-012, 12-015

Moulton, W. F., 13-016

Murphy, Roland E., 8-002

Murphy-O'Connor, Jerome., 9-017

Neirynck, F., 2-076

Nengenman, Jan H., 9-018

Nestle, E., 10-007

Newman, B. M., 12-016

Nicoll, William R., 8-034, 8-050

O'Callaghan, J., 10-003

O'Rourke, William T., 16-017

Orchard, Bernard, 14-008

Parker, J. W., 8-010

Parvis, Merril M., 2-063, 2-077

Paton, David M., 8-033

Perowne, John J. S., 8-052

Pfeiffer, C. F., 7-018

Plummer, Alfred, 8-023

Preisigke, F., 12-017

Punt, Neal R., 16-018

Quirk, Randolph, 16-019

Rea, J., 7-018

Redpath, H., 13-010

Regazzi, John J., 4-009

Richardson, Alan, 7-020, 8-033

Robertson, A. T., 11-013, 11-014

Rounds, Dorothy, 4-015

Rowley, Harold H., 8-001


Sampley, J. P., 14-004

Sayre, John L., 2-021, 4-017, 16-020,
    16-021, 16-022

Schleusner, J. F., 12-018

Schmoller, A., 13-017

Scholer, David M., 2-078

Scott, R., 12-011, 12-012, 12-013

Sheehy, Eugene P., 16-024, 16-025

Shera, Jesse H., 16-023

Shunami, Shlomo, 2-008

Simpson, David C., 8-032

Slaby, W. A., 13-002

Smith, J. B., 13-018

Smith, W., 7-021

Smith, Wilbur M., 2-009

Smyth, Kevin, 8-053

Soden, H. von, 10-008

Sophocles, E. A., 12-019

Soulen, R., 7-022

Souter, A., 12-020

Sparks, H. F. D., 8-035, 14-009

Stagenga, J., 13-019

Stegemann, H., 2-055

Steinmueller, John E., 7-023

Strack, Hermann L., 8-061

Strong, James, 13-020

Strong, Thomas B., 8-036

Strunk, William, 16-026

Swanson, R. J., 14-010


Tasker, Randolph V. G., 8-054

Tenney, M. C., 7-025, 7-026

Thackerary, H. St. J., 11-015

Thayer, J. H., 12-021

Thomas, R. L., 14-011

Thompson, W. Ralph, 8-019

Throckmorton, B. H., 14-012

Tillmann, Fritz, 8-062

Tischendorf, C., 10-009

Toomey, Alice F., 2-005

Turabian, Kate L., 16-027

Tushingham, A. D., 9-007


Van Belle, G., 2-079

Van Segbroeck, F., 2-080

Vögtle, Anton, 8-064

Vos, H. F., 7-018


Waardenburg, Jean J., 16-029

Wagner, G., 2-081

Walsh, Michael J., 2-024

Westcott, B. F., 10-010

Wigram, G. V., 13-021, 13-022

Wikenhauser, Alfred, 8-063, 8-064

Wild, Herbert, 8-036

Winkler, Paul W., 16-009

Winter, R. D., 13-023

Wright, George E., 9-019, 9-020


Yoder, J. D., 13-024

Young, Robert, 13-025


Zahn, Theodore von, 8-037

Zerwick, M., 11-016, 11-017

Zorell, F., 12-022